...LING.
...M
PLANTING

...ning
...birdbath.
...the pergola

...O TO HIRE
...FOR SOME

...olia
...cum
Blanca
..."Chameleon"
...rolina

...WOULD BE PEACEFUL.
...T A GARDEN AT THE
...GE
...ULD BE PERFECT FOR
...NING

How do I make my garden attractive in the winter?

It is important to be familiar with the spirit of your garden — this is known as the Genius Loci. So get outside & walk about, peer into every corner. If possible, try to spend one full cycle of seasons gazing at & spending time in your garden. These are serious musings, as they will tell you what kind of garden will serve you well.

I would love a water garden

What equipment do I need?

- GLOVES · TRANSPLANTING SPADE
- TROWEL WITH AN EXTRA LONG DISH
- GOOD PAIR OF SECATEURS
- LOPPERS · GARDEN SHEARS
- SMALL WOODEN RAKE.

WHAT DO I WANT AS MY FOCAL POINT?

How to Make a Garden
The 7 Essential Steps for the Canadian Gardener

Marjorie Harris

How to Make a Garden
The 7 Essential Steps for the Canadian Gardener

An Angel Edition
for
Random House Canada

www.randomhouse.ca

Library and Archives Canada Cataloguing in Publication

Harris, Marjorie
        How to make a garden : the 7 essential steps for
the Canadian gardener / Marjorie Harris.

Includes index.
ISBN-13: 978-0-679-31448-6
ISBN-10: 0-679-31448-2

        1. Gardening—Canada. I. Title.

SB453.3.C2H374 2007   635'.0971   c2006-903281-5

Jacket and Text Design: Underline Studio

Printed and bound in Singapore

10 9 8 7 6 5 4 3 2 1

Contents

Introduction

To be at work in the garden is at the core of my life. It is my passion and has dominated my work since I started writing about gardening in the 1980s. But it wasn't a simple journey. When I started in 1967, I knew almost nothing about gardening. My urban backyard was completely intimidating; filled with weeds, it seemed huge (19 by 100 feet), and all I could identify were some struggling old peonies.

We all start out this way: fearful at the responsibility. It's a little like having a baby and not being quite sure how to look after it. So often, our gardens are tabula rasa and it's up to us to fill them with grace and style. Although I felt it was too much for me to handle, I learned to conquer these fears and to build the garden slowly.

"This book is for people who are baffled by empty space… but it's also for people who have lovely gardens…"

Previous spread: A view of my garden in full bloom.

Doing what I now call pregardening, I knew enough to clean up the space just to see what was there—I found lots of little treasures. Decades earlier, someone had obviously loved this space. Not only were there peonies, but also self-seeding forget-me-nots that still grace the garden in their unique way every spring. And there was the detritus once normal for all city gardens: ashes from the furnace, buried construction junk, ancient bottles and crockery, abandoned children's toys. Since the back wall of our house is all windows overlooking the garden, I had no choice but to fix it up. I learned what to do by flailing around outside and keeping track of everything I did. These notes eventually evolved into the books I've written.

To make any kind of garden takes time, and that's something I didn't understand at the beginning. I thought if you clean it up, put in some plants and mow the lawn, you'll have a wonderful garden. Alas, no. The more I found out about gardening the better I wanted to make the garden look. I acquired the divine discontent that all crazed gardeners possess. I loved my garden, but surely it could look better than this? I thought a couple of seasons of planting would do it, but it was many years before I could safely say: This is what I was aiming for.

In the 1980s, I got fed up with how boring my garden looked and started going at it in a more methodical way. I had lots of notes about light; I knew I had good soil, so why was my garden so unsatisfying? I finally realized that I had no overall design, no vision behind what I was doing. So I stopped and just spent an entire winter staring at my garden, creative staring as it turned out.

By spring, after doing masses of drawings, I was armed with a plan, a garden map and a budget—all necessary elements in making a garden. I came up with the checkerboard pattern of paving stones that became the underpinning of the garden and had it installed by a brilliant young gardener. He was the one who suggested making a berm (a long raised bed) out of all the soil we had removed. What he built was scaled perfectly to the size of the garden. I learned a lot from him about gardening. And I learned that there are times when a professional is not only the best investment you can make, but also the only sensible solution to a problem.

This book is for people (like me in 1967) who are baffled by empty space, cowed by weeds and longing to have something gorgeous to look at. But it's also for people (like me now) who have lovely gardens but need to be reminded of the basics in garden-building, the core ideas that make a garden truly successful.

During the writing of this book, we added a garden room to the back of the house and my perspective on the garden changed. Like a game of chess, one move leads to many more. In this case, a newly installed fountain sculpture made the checkerboard feel redundant. After twenty plus years of its company, I felt vaguely disloyal at taking the checkerboard out; but I did, making space for more plants to complement the fountain. Other plants will have to be moved as I settle into this new design, but that's part of the fun. And now I know I don't have to rush for instant effect. I can leave things as they are for a year and see every little fault reveal itself. Then I will tackle them one at a time.

Nothing about gardening panics me any more except the possibility that global climate change is going to affect the kinds of plants that grow best in our area. Or that planting something four years in a row and having it fail every time might be a message that I can't grow everything even though my spirit is willing to try.

I love growing older in my garden. It's maturing along with me and is always changing, something I hope for in myself as well. You cannot touch a garden without being touched by it in a profound way. We are the stewards of such a small space on this planet, and we should make sure we leave it better than we found it. Gardening changed my life from being merely interesting into something ecstatic. And it can do the same for you.

How do I deal with different types of light in my garden?

morning sun

only shady plants

EVENING SUN

WILL PLANTS GROW IN MY CURRENT SOIL?

Are the outdoor taps convenient to use?

Can I work with the steep slope in my yard?

HOW FAR WILL MY BUDGET stretch?

$ $ $

Step One

Become a Pregardener

Survey Your Site
Determine Your Quality of Light
Check Your Water Supply
Learn Gardening Terms
Consider Your Budget
Essential Pregardening Tasks
The Pregardening Garden

Become a Pregardener

This was the beginning of my own small downtown garden, back in the 1980s. The checkerboard design provided organization for a disorganized gardener and radiant warmth for the new plants, as well as plenty of room for large borders on either side.

WHETHER YOU ARE FACING a blank suburban square of grass or an old, overgrown city plot, there is no site that can't be changed for the better. Gardening is all about balance: creating shady patches and hot spots, combining exuberant jungles and tailored edges, making social areas and solitary spaces, planting tall trees and delicate ground covers. To create this mosaic requires some thought, and that's the first thing to understand before you even begin to build a new garden—call it pregardening.

It's important to become familiar with the feel or spirit of your garden—this is known as the *genius loci*—so get outside and walk about, peer into every corner. If possible, try to spend one cycle of seasons gazing at and spending time in your yard to assess light levels, rain patterns, soil types and what plants are already there before you make a move. Contemplation can go a long way toward the making of a garden. But first, like any painter facing a blank canvas, you need to know what kind of artist you are. Have you always had a secret passion for gardening but never had a space to make your own until now? Are you the type who can't wait for nature, who wants instant results with truckloads of soil, giant rocks and plenty of minions to do your bidding? Are you a lawn worshipper with visions of putting-green velvet? Or are you a director rather than an actor, i.e., someone who would rather hire the help than do the work?

Perhaps you're someone who is incredibly busy with other priorities (work, children) that will get in the way of spending time in the garden. Ask yourself if you are a nervous Nellie who will start the garden but never finish it, or a person who will dig in and relish every moment in the dirt.

These are serious musings because they tell you what kind of garden will serve you well and spare you the frustration of over-reaching dreams. Ruthless honesty is an absolute necessity. Knowing yourself and your needs will help you build a garden that is right for you (just like finding the perfect house or spouse).

Pregardening Basics

While you are contemplating your garden, there are a few things you need to assess.

Survey Your Site Look at the topography of your site. Assess the potential problems or possibilities of features such as steep slopes, low-lying areas where water collects, or rocky outcrops with no soil. Sometimes if you have lemons, you have to make lemonade. A steep slope may not make a children's playground, but it could be a spectacular terraced garden. A depression could become a lovely pond. Are there immovable objects you will have to take into account such as fire hydrants and air-conditioning units? Are there wonderful features such as a natural stream or rock formation that you love and want to incorporate in the garden? Consider practicalities such as a gas line for a barbecue or fireplace, and electrical outlets for lighting, pond pumps and the like. It's best to deal with these things before you plant or build anything. Retrofitting is always expensive.

Determine Your Quality of Light Gardening is about light and it will take at least one summer to understand what light your garden receives. If it gets six hours of sun or more, that is considered "full sun." "Part sun" means that a garden gets five to six hours of sunshine a day. "Part shade" means four hours of sun a day. If your garden enjoys only early-morning sun, you've got shade most of the day. Late-afternoon sun also means a lot of shade, but the sun you do get is much stronger. A south-facing slope can get hot and dry, while a north-facing slope will be cool and shady.

The types of shade a garden has is significant because each kind supports different plants. Is the shade light, high, dappled or deep? Light shade means the area is bright but not in full sun; high shade and dappled shade refer to the shade found under tree canopies or structures that allow light to filter through; and deep shade means that area on the north side of the house where the sun doesn't shine. Bear in mind that over winter deciduous trees are bare, so if you have a large maple tree you will have sun in early spring but shade once the tree leafs out. Note other elements that can affect the light in your garden: neighbouring trees, fences, hedges and nearby buildings (their walls can block or bounce light something fierce).

Top left: My garden as it is today, grown up and filled in with many layers and with plants to make a gorgeous scene each season.
Bottom left: My garden in winter, after 15 years of adding and subtracting. It shows how many good winter plants you can add to a small garden without it looking crowded.

"Think about what you can afford to put into the first stage of your garden."

I measured the light in my garden by making a sun map: I divided the garden into sections and marked down the number of hours the sun hit each section at the summer solstice (around June 21), and again at the autumn equinox (around September 23). Then, for each part of the garden, I added the summer and autumn numbers together and divided that total in half to get a good idea of the amount of light coming in. From there, it was easy to determine whether each area is full sun, part shade, part sun, etc. For example, if one section received nine hours of sunlight in June and five in September the total is fourteen hours. That figure divided in half is seven, so the section would be considered a full-sun area.

Check Your Water Supply Water is a critical element for plants, but you don't want too much or too little. Look at rainfall patterns, and see where the dry spots and wet spots are. Whacking great puddles mean you have drainage problems, which must be solved before building any garden. I have the lowest garden in my neighbourhood so I dug a dry well and put in a sump pump to slow down the annual spring flood. The sump pump is attached to a hose that directs water into the sewer system.

Check to see where your outdoor taps are and how conveniently they are placed; double spigots will allow you to run two hoses from one outlet, handy for watering more than one area at a time. Think about relocating inconveniently placed taps—it's not hugely expensive and is labour-saving in the long term. If you have a large property or are away from home a lot, consider including an irrigation system in your garden plan.

Learn Gardening Terms The more you work on planning your garden (reading books and magazines, talking to experts and nursery staff, and searching the Internet), the more you'll come across gardening vocabulary. Here are some terms that you should know:

HARDSCAPING is a design term referring to all the hard elements such as pathways, patios, rocks, ponds and fountains, fences, walls, arbours, screens and items such as sculptures, planters and furnishings.

SOFTSCAPING refers to all plants:

Perennials are plants that come back year after year. Some, like peonies, can live for a hundred years; others may last only a few.

Annuals give colour and instant effect because they bloom, go to seed and die in one year. They are incredibly useful plants but a garden composed entirely of annuals looks boring and costs the earth because you must start from scratch every year.

Woody plants are trees, shrubs and perennials with woody stems that don't disappear in winter. These indispensable plants give the garden its "bones," or its year-round form and underlying structure.

BORDERS are planting beds. They can be any shape and don't have to be located on the perimeter of your garden. Borders can run the length of a fence, extend around a corner, or be free-standing in the middle of the lawn (an island border—these things have no logic).

RAISED BEDS are planting beds built up higher than the overall soil level; they are often used for herbs, vegetables and plants requiring special growing conditions.

A FOCAL POINT is an intriguing object or feature, such as a statue, fountain, statuesque plant or pond, that can be seen from a distance and draws you into the garden.

Consider Your Budget Think about what you can afford to put into the first stage of your garden. Don't kid yourself about this. Just as you would guesstimate costs before redecorating your house, do some homework and get an idea of what various garden elements cost so you will be able to set a realistic budget. Total cost depends on the quality you buy; for example, a handsome wooden fence might cost from $3,000 to $15,000 depending on the size of the garden, but you could opt for a chain-link fence and cover it with vines for substantially less. Any large item, such as a deck or pond and waterfall, is going to be costly—$5,000 to $10,000 for each is a minimum gardening rule of thumb.

Consider, too, how much of the work you are prepared to do yourself and what you will have to pay someone for—from the heavy-duty, specialized tasks such as laying a stone terrace to expert advice regarding trees, lighting, design, installing gas lines, electrical outlets and an irrigation system, etc. Design help will cost from $60 to $100 an hour, while a consultation with a professional landscape architect could run $1,000 or more. Also, replacing and replenishing your soil could cost from $300 to $3,000 if you pay someone to do it. On the other hand, for next to nothing, you can cover the soil you have with well-rotted manure and chopped-up leaves and let it lie fallow for a year; this is the route I took with sections of my own garden.

Think about what aspects of your garden-building you can realistically do yourself (would you consider building a deck, laying paving stones and planting trees?). For heavy-duty tasks, keep in mind that professionals come with yard machinery so they can dig and move rocks and heavy soil around in half the time you could. They may not be as cheap as if you did the work, but things will get done effectively. If you do need expert help such as a garden designer, arbourist, pond specialist or lighting designer, get a recommended one who has some previous work to show. Make sure you look at two other gardens they've done and, when the time comes, listen to what they have to say. For example, I hired a wonderful lighting designer and once the first round was done, I felt there was a bit too much light in the middle of the design. She removed the bulbs to let me live with it. Two days later, I realized she was absolutely right; the bulbs went back in.

To find a good professional, do some research: attend local garden shows where many pros have exhibits or booths, and pick up their literature. Consult horticultural organizations such as those devoted to native plants and rooftop gardens as well as individual plant societies such as the Ontario Daylily Society and the Canadian Peony Society for designers who specialize in the style you've chosen. Also, check the membership lists of provincial landscape associations. I think, however, the best way is to go on garden tours, look for work that you like and ask a lot of questions.

Top left: A good interior screen provides privacy and support for decoration.
Top right: A raised bed provides warmth for plants in colder climates and makes a sitting area. Dwarf conifers and other rockery plants add great colour and texture year round.
Bottom: Every garden needs a focal point like this statue. It draws the eye and enhances the choice of surrounding plants.

Above, from left: This fence is perfect for the relaxed style of a country garden. The wattling, made by the owner, was created from material found around the property; a cement bench with the right kind of background (this one is surrounded by coreopsis) is an inviting place to sit; every garden needs a place to eat *alfresco*—in this garden the horizontal fence and interior screen give the space a cosseted feel; a simple but elegant water feature will attract birds and insects and mask the sounds of the city.

When making your budget, think long range. Remember that prices go up every year so be practical about money and proceed a step at a time as you can afford it. Don't try to do everything at once or you'll get discouraged. Decide whether you are going to deal with the entire property (front and back) or only part of it. You might want to concentrate on the most private space (usually the backyard), and leave the rest until you feel really confident.

Here's a list of items that you will need to budget for:

- Rock or soil removal and clearing of the ground
- Replacement soil plus amendments such as sand and compost
- Stonework for walls and paths, such as bricks, gravel and pavers
- Patios and decks
- Fences, screens, trellises, gates and a storage shed
- Furnishings including a table, chairs and umbrella
- Water features
- Lighting
- Containers
- Plants: This cost will vary according to how many trees you plant. Trees can cost from $200 each for small ones to several thousand dollars for mature specimens, which should be installed by a professional who will guarantee them for at least a year. Shrubs will cost from $30 to $150 (I recommend you plant your own). Perennials cost from $4 up to $100 each depending on their quality and how

rare they are; annuals are cheaper but last only a season. Bulbs are generally a bargain—most not only return every year but also multiply all by themselves. For the first year, I suggest you allot 60 percent of your total plant budget for trees (at least two) and shrubs; and 40 percent for perennials, annuals and bulbs. Subsequently, you will probably need fewer woody plants and can focus more on perennials, annuals and bulbs.

Essential Pregardening Tasks

While you are determining the pregardening basics, get out into your space to find out exactly what you have to work with. In the process, make it as attractive as possible by following these steps:

Tidy Up This sounds simple enough but it means getting rid of that dilapidated shed (you can't save it), the junk that's been thrown in the back during renovating, the inexplicable piles of wood. Make the space as blank a canvas as possible before you consider how you want your garden to look.

Remove as many weeds as you can. They spring up even in hard clay soil. You can solarize the weediest areas: lay a sheet of dark plastic over the area, weight the edges, and leave it for a couple of weeks in the hot summer sun. The weeds underneath will fry to death.

"Don't know what you have or if it's worth keeping? Call in an expert to help you with identification and assessment."

Be Wary of Removing Trees Don't take out trees before you have a chance to see their effect on the garden. Removing a big old tree will bring sun where there was shade, but will the sacrifice be worth it? There are such things as weed trees (Manitoba maple, tree of heaven, Chinese elm) and you should get rid of them, as well as any dying or diseased trees.

Don't know what you have or if it's worth keeping? Call in an expert from your local nursery or a professional arbourist to help you with identification and assessment. If you are lucky enough to have healthy mature trees—they lend solidity to a new garden—hire an arbourist to prune them. A good arbourist will clean out dead or dangerous branches and remove lower limbs (called limbing up) to let more light into the garden without losing the natural canopy. This process isn't cheap but it pays off handsomely.

Every garden should include some evergreens; they add permanent structure, provide colour and texture in winter, and offer habitat for birds. If you have some evergreens already, make certain they are healthy. If they aren't, take them out and plan for new ones.

Don't Be Sentimental About Plants You don't have to keep every existing plant just because it's there. If you see something you really hate the look of after seeing it in all seasons, take it out. My *bête noire* was a ratty-looking spirea, which I removed to make way for two wonderful shrubs—'Summer Snowflake' viburnum and red-leaf rose— that I still love decades later. If you get an expert in to help identify plants and he or she recommends tearing something out, do it. Similarly, listen to any advice about keeping plants that could be valuable in your new garden (a rare old lilac cultivar or unusual evergreen, for example).

Start Feeding Your Soil Begin to enrich the soil in any areas you think you will want to plant. A useful fall/winter project is to collect fallen leaves, buy bagged compost or manure, and dump everything in alternating layers over the future planting area, then let it sit over winter.

Deciduous Trees

Don't remove deciduous trees from your garden. Although they lose their leaves each fall, they are wonderful for spring and summer shade and shape. In the winter they offer good structure for your garden. If you don't currently have a deciduous tree, try to choose one native to your region. I have a Kentucky coffee tree (Gymnocladus dioica), which I really love for its entrancing enormous leaves that have become a focal point of the garden.

Remove Eyesores If there is an unavoidable eyesore in your garden (such as a parking area), put up an attractive screen to hide it just as you might conceal a work area in the house. You can buy a screen or make it yourself. Let it be simple, elegant (large square lattice is perfect) and, for the time being, portable. It may have to be moved once garden creation begins in earnest.

The Pregardening Garden

If you really hanker to do something as you dream about your ultimate garden, consider doing the following. This pregardening garden will provide some immediate gratification, a glimpse of the possibilities ahead, and some hands-on learning (see step 6 for specific planting instructions). None of these plants will go to waste, and if you make a mistake or change your mind in a year they can still be moved.

Plant a Native Shrub or Tree A shrub such as serviceberry (*Amelanchier* spp.) will provide year-round interest, make a good screen, and create an excellent habitat for wildlife. If you are confident that you know where a larger tree is going to go, plant one native to your area. I'm talking about a tree that will grow large since most young trees at the nursery are 10 feet (3 metres) tall or less at the time of sale. It will take years for this tree to reach a substantial size and in the meantime you will have the pleasure of its company. For additional impact, place a small decorative tree such as a Japanese maple (*Acer palmatum*) within 10 feet (3 metres) of the larger one. If Japanese maples aren't hardy in your area, try a dwarf birch (*Betula* spp.), cutleaf elder (*Sambucus* spp.) or sumac (*Rhus* 'Tiger Eyes')—they all have seductive leaves and a gorgeous shape.

Plant a Range of Vines Place clematis, virginia creeper or annual morning glories on any bare fence, shed or other structure you have. My favourite vine is sweet autumn clematis (*Clematis terniflora*); it grows like mad and produces cascades of creamy flowers in fall.

Above, from left:
Amelanchier spp. has different names in different parts of the country—I know it as the serviceberry and it is one of my all-time favourite plants; a clematis 'Ville de Lyon' growing up a lattice screen; a wonderful way to experiment with plants and to try out new colour combinations is to use only one type of plant in each container—in this case tulips and narcissus, which make a vibrant edge to a border.

Try Out Plants in Small Planting Beds and Pots Start to experiment but keep it simple and pay attention to foliage as much as flowers. Good colour combinations are blue and white; purple and magenta; lime green and burgundy. Just don't dot one plant here and one there in a confetti effect; plant in groups of at least three, or in irregular drifts (large groups). Put in at least two ornamental grasses for autumn and winter interest. Plant containers with annuals and/or perennials and move them around your space to gauge the different effects you can achieve with colour.

There is a lot to learn when creating a garden, but remember that you are in charge, and your choices will ultimately define the space. Gardening is very much like homemaking: use a little common sense, some organization and a good deal of taste and you'll end up with something pretty wonderful. If you make a planting mistake, it's relatively easy to change things in the early years without a lot of expense or effort.

The important thing is to take the time to find out your needs, discover what the garden offers in the way of light, soil and space, and

work out an overall plan that you can implement in stages. That way you'll avoid major errors such as putting a pond in the wrong spot, or buying a lot of rocks that are all wrong for your design.

No matter how much a garden changes, however, there is always one important basic: minding your soil. It is such a significant factor in good gardening, it merits a step of its own. Good soil is a must even in pregardening.

Straw mulch

Sandy soil

Leaf mulch

Cedar mulch

Sandy Loam soil

Cocoa fibre mulch

Clay soil

Know Your Soil

Soil Types
Soil Testing
Drainage
Soil Amending
New Soil
Soil Secrets
Composting
Mulching

Know Your Soil

Soil is the soul of gardening—it should smell sweet and look like the friable mixture illustrated here. Soil that's ready to plant in is loose, with lots of humus (organic matter) and just the right mix of nutrients to stimulate growth. By contrast, compacted soil will look hard and dead.

YOU HAVE FAMILIARIZED YOURSELF with your space and thought about its potential, but before going to the next step it's wise to look at what is basic to all gardening, indeed to life itself: the soil. Soil is the first thing to begin with when building a new garden. Without good soil, forget about good gardening. To know your soil is to establish a relationship with one of the most important elements on this planet. Soil is a living organism, a complex ecosystem comprised of billions of bacteria, nematodes, protozoa, earthworms and millions of other living creatures all working, farming and procreating all the time. They toil away breaking down organic matter, producing nutrients that feed the plants. All this activity, together with air and water, which make up 50 percent of soil, makes it friable (easy for roots to penetrate and easy to dig in).

Soils high in organic matter (decomposing plant and animal material) and humus (the final result of the process) are the liveliest, healthiest soils. They are full of the principal nutrients (nitrogen, phosphorus and potassium), as well as secondary nutrients and trace minerals. Vital to all plants, nitrogen stimulates leaf and stem growth; phosphorus is important for root development and the production of fruit and flowers; and potassium promotes overall vigour and disease resistance.

The Elements of Soil

Constantly absorbing and recycling, soil handles a lot: fallen leaves, insect and bird droppings, dead trees, even dead animals. (Like many gardens, mine is a repository for all the mice and gerbils, now long expired, that were brought home from school, and who knows how many other creatures that have decomposed unseen by human eyes. It's all part of a natural process.) If we tidy our gardens too much, picking up every last twig and seed pod, we risk messing up this balance. It's much better to join the circle of nature. With excellent soil you'll be able to garden without any worries for about fifteen years—indefinitely if you feed it regularly and keep it healthy. Treat soil like dirt and you'll run into problems almost immediately. Knowing the soil basics will help you work with what you have.

Top left: Very loose soil usually means that there's a lot of sand in it and that the drainage will be very sharp (meaning speedy).
Top right: Sandy loam is the most highly desirable soil, with just enough humus to feed plants as they need it.
Bottom: Heavy clay soil is full of nutrients but it usually has terrible drainage. It needs the addition of lots of sand and humus to lighten its texture.

Soil Types

Sandy soil has a pale look with large soil particles that feel gritty. Water flows through it quickly, which makes for excellent drainage but also means it doesn't hold nutrients well. Clay soil is made up of tiny, tightly packed particles and tends to be difficult to dig, but it holds water well and is high in nutrients. Pick up a handful of damp soil, squeeze it and then open your hand. If it runs through your fingers, you've got sandy soil; if it holds its shape, you've got clay. Between these two extremes there are many different kinds of soil, but the stuff at the centre of the spectrum is the ideal: sandy loam. Perfect for most plants, sandy loam is dark and crumbly like a chocolate cake and has the nutrient richness of clay together with the easy drainage of sand. It is often found in river valleys and prime agricultural land. The soil in your garden will likely be quite consistent unless your property is larger than an acre and has a varied topography (woods, ponds, hills, etc.).

Soil Testing

To determine your soil's fertility, as well as the degree of acidity or alkalinity (called pH), you should have an analysis done. Dig 4-inch (10-centimetre) holes in several places around the garden, take a tablespoon (15 millilitres) or so of soil from each, combine them, put the mixture into a container, and send it off to a soil-testing laboratory. Home soil-testing kits are also available from your local garden centre. The results can tell you what major nutrients are present or lacking and your soil's pH level. The pH level of soil determines how easily plants can take up nutrients. The pH scale runs from 1 (most acid) to 14 (most alkaline); most plants like it right in the middle, around 7.

If you have very alkaline soil (pH 7.5 or higher), you will have trouble growing plants that prefer a slightly acidic soil, such as rhododendrons. You will often read about adding peat moss to increase soil acidity, and lime to increase alkalinity, but don't bother. It would take years to significantly change soil pH. Better to add lots of compost, which will help to moderate the pH either way, and grow plants that suit your conditions.

Drainage

All plants (with the exception of water plants) need good drainage; if their roots are sitting in water, they will drown. To test your drainage, dig a hole 12 inches (30 centimetres) deep, fill it with water and watch what happens. If the water disappears almost immediately, your soil has high

"Regular applications of organic matter will both build and maintain good soil."

sand content and won't hold adequate moisture for the plant roots. If the water takes three to six hours to drain away, you have good drainage. Longer than six hours means you have poor drainage, which could result in waterlogged roots. Amending the soil will improve drainage.

Soil Amending

Amending the soil (primarily by adding organic matter) is an ongoing process and prepares it to withstand potential problems such as drought (good soil holds water better) and compaction (good soil is loose and friable). Apart from material such as leaves, compost and well-rotted manure, little else needs to be added to maintain soil health.

Amendments don't need to be mixed into the soil. Just spread them on the surface (this is called top-dressing) when you are preparing a planting bed and a couple of times a year after that; I usually do it in spring and fall. The rain will filter nutrients through and the valiant earthworms will pull all the leaves and stuff underground. If you are adding nutrients such as phosphorus and trace minerals (found in powdered rock phosphate), do it in late autumn before snow falls; they will be gradually absorbed over the winter.

Regular applications of organic matter (see the section on mulching, page 39) will both build and maintain good soil. I find it easier to tackle one section of the garden at a time but if you have a small garden less than 25 feet (7.6 metres) square, you can do it all at once. You'll know that you are amending your soil properly when you see how well the plants respond.

AMENDING SANDY SOIL To improve sandy soil, add a layer of organic matter about 2 inches (5 centimetres) deep over the entire surface. Organic matter comprises leaves, shrub clippings, fallen tree branches, shredded bark, etc. You don't have to dig it in; let it break down slowly.

AMENDING CLAY SOIL Adding organic matter will improve clay soils, too. You can also pile on coarse sand (the type used to make concrete) to a depth of 3 inches (7.5 centimetres). It will look like a desert at the start

but the sand will sink in quite quickly. Later, when you have your garden planted, you can cover the area around the plants with a mixture of coarse grit and fine horticultural sand (a fine-grade sand available at nurseries or landscape supply stores). If you've read about adding triple mix to clay soil, don't bother; most triple mixes contain clay and you don't want to be adding more. It's a better addition to sandy soils.

New Soil

If you have to bring in new soil to your garden (to build new planting areas or replace topsoil that has been carted away), find a reliable company that guarantees the contents of its product. Someone there will calculate how many yards of soil you need to buy based on the area you want to cover and the depth of soil required. Be sure you have an accessible place where the soil can be dumped either by the truckload or by the giant bag.

Watch out for stuff advertised as "clean fill." This may be soil, but could also be gravel and stones. Don't buy anything scooped out of a cornfield; it will be filled with chemicals and weeds—and telltale bits of corncobs.

Soil Secrets

The formula for superb soil is a simple one: give it some TLC, feed it with compost, protect it with mulch, then leave it alone.

Soil is a living thing and should be treated with care. Avoid running heavy equipment over it or even treading on it a lot, especially when it's wet. This compacts soil, compressing the spaces between its particles and driving out vital air and water. Have a board or a piece of rigid plastic to stand or kneel on when you have a lot of planting to do; this distributes your weight more widely. Don't cultivate your soil with a garden fork or rototiller as this will only disturb the complex relationships of the soil ecosystem. Don't poison it with toxic herbicides and insecticides that kill not only the so-called pests but also all the beneficial organisms that work so hard to keep the soil healthy. Pesticide use carries the risk of contaminating the ground water, as well as affecting you, your children

"Weapons on your side: compost and mulch."

and your animals. Keep your soil evenly moist; don't let it bake and dry out, or get waterlogged. Make the care and feeding of your soil part of your regular maintenance program; it takes time to "grow" fabulous soil, but your plants will thank you for it.

As an organic gardener and a good steward of the soil, you have two major natural weapons on your side: compost and mulch. Compost is made from organic matter that breaks down over a matter of months to form a micro-organism-rich soil conditioner. You can place a layer of compost around ailing plants to give them a boost and also use it as part of your mulch mixture. Mulch is a protective blanket of organic matter on the soil surface that moderates the temperature, holds in water, discourages weeds, and prevents erosion and compaction. Mulch is usually a combination of organic materials including compost, ground-up leaves, straw, shredded bark and manure. (Well-composted manure doesn't smell. If you buy manure that does smell, return it to the supplier. Don't use fresh manure in your garden; besides being very pungent, it will burn the plants.) Compost is absorbed into the soil very quickly; mulch lasts much longer because the materials are still in the process of breaking down.

Composting

Making compost involves taking all the organic stuff from the garden and kitchen, putting it in a big pile, and letting it break down. It's an ongoing thing: you just keep adding to the pile, turn it every week and, over several months, it decomposes and turns into the most beautiful black soil-like material. I'm a big believer in composting. In the decades I've been working the same plot I've never added anything to it but compost.

The process of composting creates a great deal of heat, killing off weed seeds and speeding up decomposition. It also shrinks the raw material, so what may start off as a pile 3 feet (90 centimetres) high ends up as a medium-sized basket of rich compost. Keep this in mind: a layer of compost spread 2 inches (5 centimetres) deep on the ground provides enough nitrogen, a nutrient vital to plant growth, for more than a year.

Compost should be made from all the kitchen scraps you can gather—though nothing with any protein (no butter, no rice). Chop up the scraps finely, then use as one layer of the compost. The other layer comes from all the weeds and small bits of green detritus from around the garden.

Above, from left: Smaller, plastic composters like this one are okay if they are all you can accommodate; if you have more room, a large-sized wooden composter like the one in my garden is ideal—it has removable slats in the front so it's easy to turn over the compost; leaves should never be tossed out, they are an essential component of compost and have all the nutrients plants need; store leaves in larger containers wherever you have the room.

HOW TO COMPOST You will need a lidded bin large enough so the pile will heat up properly. The optimum size is 4 feet by 4 feet by 4 feet (1.2 by 1.2 by 1.2 metres). It can be made of wood slats or metal mesh, but there needs to be some air circulation. If you don't have room for one that size, get the largest commercial composter you can.

Add the material in layers of green (moist) and brown (dry). Green is stuff such as grass clippings, shrub and perennial clippings, weeds without seeds, and kitchen scraps; brown stuff is dry leaves, small twigs, pine needles, sawdust, dryer lint and paper including newsprint, paper towels and coffee filters. By kitchen scraps I mean fruit and vegetable parings, coffee grounds, tea bags, pasta (no sauce), bread and eggshells. Never, ever, add leftovers from meals or anything that contains protein (meat, eggs or dairy), fats or oils, pet droppings or toxic plants such as poison ivy. Chop up the raw material, to about the size of a toonie if possible. You don't have to add worms—start a compost bin and red wrigglers will come, along with a lot of other worms and little bugs. Don't worry about them; they are working for you.

Turn the compost every week or so. This aerates it and moves the organisms around, accelerating decomposition. You can also add manure to speed things up (sheep, horse, chicken, cow or mushroom, in that order) or seaweed if it's available to you. Throw in a layer of soil or manure occasionally to prevent smells and give the pile a boost of micro-organisms. If turned regularly, the compost should be finished in six weeks or so; three months if not turned. Keep the compost moist, spraying it with the hose if needed. If the compost gets too wet from heavy rain or too many green additions, it will be soggy and smelly; and if it's too dry, it will attract ants rather than all the little creatures you need.

You can use compost even if it's not quite finished. Just run it through a sieve, tossing any worms and large bits that don't go through

Composting Techniques

Alternate layers of green (kitchen and garden waste) and brown (dried leaves, manure) into the composter. Make sure it's as wet as a squeezed out sponge at all times. Turn it every few days—this is crucial to keep oxygen flowing and to make the temperature rise. Stick your hand into the mix, or get a thermometer if you must and see if the middle of the mixture is hot. If not keep turning the mix over and keep moistening.

the sieve back into the compost pile. If the bin is quite full, the compost will continue to cook no matter what the temperature is outside. You can burrow a hole in the middle of the pile and add kitchen scraps all winter long; that will keep the worms fed. Once frost arrives, put garbage bags full of leaves on top of the compost pile to keep it warm and active.

FALLEN LEAVES A primary ingredient in both compost and mulch, leaves are an incredibly valuable resource—and they're free. Left alone, they will form a natural mulch, gradually breaking down into the soil. However, large leaves such as those from a Norway maple can form an impenetrable mat and keep moisture from percolating through the soil. Rake those up, as well as any leaves on the lawn—they will smother the grass if left. Compost them or chop them up and spread them around trees and shrubs.

In the fall, bag up some leaves in black garbage bags and toss in a little soil with a bit of compost added. Kick the bags around occasionally to stir things up and store near the composter for the winter. They will be handy when you need some brown material to top up the compost pile. Bags of leaves also make ideal protection for large perennial-filled containers.

Pick up any mouldy fruit and blighted leaves with brown, red or black spots that could indicate fungal diseases. Remove them from the garden, but don't put them into the composter. Fungi will winter over on leaves and fruit left on the ground and will re-infect your plants the following season.

Mulching

If there is a magic bullet in gardening, it's mulching twice a year: in the early winter and spring. Mulch is a cosy blanket of organic matter such as leaves, straw or bark that protects the soil. The forest floor is

The Mulch Trap

Bugs love mulch because it's a cool safe place to bed down in. Think of it as a slug and earwig trap.

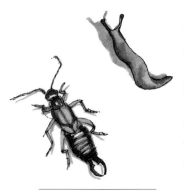

naturally full of leaf litter and dead plants, with no tidy gardeners to clean it up. Without that protective covering, soil becomes dry, compacted, weedy and subject to drastic temperature changes, not the ideal environment for plants. Mulch keeps the soil temperature stable, insulates root systems, holds in moisture, and keeps soil from being pummelled by rain, wind and cold.

In summer, mulch holds down the growth of weeds while allowing rain or water to filter through to the soil below. In winter, mulch helps to protect plants from heaving. This happens when the soil freezes, thaws, then freezes again. Water in the soil expands and contracts, heaving plants right out of the ground.

Inorganic mulches, such as stones and gravel, are useful in rock gardens, xeriscapes (dry-land gardens) and containers. They discourage squirrels and slugs and do provide a few minerals to the soil. However, organic mulches such as leaf mould and shredded bark are better because they encourage all those micro-organisms to multiply and supply the soil with nutrients. If you use an inorganic mulch, pour a good compost tea over it regularly. To make compost tea: put one part finished compost into a burlap bag and let it steep in six parts of water for a week. Dilute to half strength with water and pour over the area.

HOW TO MULCH Winter mulch should be applied once there is hard frost in the ground. Hard frost is observable: you'll come out one morning and everything will be lined with white, any water will be ice. The ground freezes when the frost moves down into lower layers of the soil. Spread winter mulch at least 2 inches (5 centimetres) thick; 4 inches (10 centimetres) is best for complete protection. In spring, to let the soil warm up more quickly, scrape off most of the mulch and toss it into the composter. Add a layer of compost to the soil to feed it and top it off with a generous layer of spring mulch, preferably an organic type, at least 2 inches (5 centimetres) deep. You'll be astounded at how your plants will thrive.

Don't sprinkle mulch around as though it's expensive perfume. Better to apply it thickly between major or vulnerable plants than spread

Straw has a hollow core so it makes for really good insulation as a winter mulch. It does have one problem: it looks terrible. By spring little will have broken down and you can scrape it off and put it in the compost. But it is slow. If you have a pebble mulch, put a layer of straw about a foot below the surface when you are planting and over time it will break down into organic matter, feeding the root system of the plants.

it in a parsimonious manner. Never push mulch up against stems or the crowns of plants. Leave a gap of about 3 inches (7.5 centimetres) to give the plant some air and keep stems from rotting. Spread mulch around newly planted trees and shrubs right out to the drip line (the area covered by the tree's canopy) to a depth of 4 inches (10 centimetres), remembering to keep it away from the trunks.

You can also try two ways of mini-mulching. The first, forest floor mulching, involves chopping up spent plant stalks and scattering the bits over flower beds. The second is simply to use a mulching mower and leave fresh grass clippings on the lawn; they are a good source of nitrogen and will break down quickly. (Too thick a layer of grass clippings piled in the composter will smell bad very quickly because they start decomposing without oxygen.)

Mulch is viewed by various bugs and critters as the ideal spa in which to spend the summer. You, on the other hand, have to think of it as a place in which to trap the little devils. This attitude will help when you find masses of slugs and earwigs in there. Just squish them underfoot and get on with gardening.

TYPES OF ORGANIC MULCHES The best mulches include compost but few gardeners have that in sufficient quantity without buying commercial products or getting some from local composting programs (most municipalities have them). The problem is that much municipal compost comes from piles of leaves gathered from roadsides and contains salt and

Above, clockwise from top left: Coir is a renewable resource that is far more effective than peat moss in holding moisture in the soil. Use it with other organic materials; leaves are one of the best ground covers. They contain all the right minerals and break down easily once they are ground up; straw is a very good insulator, though not particularly aesthetically pleasing; cedar bark makes a nice ground cover if, like this, it's finely milled. Don't use the great big chunks.

possibly other chemicals. You do not want to spread this around vegetables. To get around this dilemma I strongly recommend that you buy or make mulch. All the mulches listed here will do the trick. Go with what's available and what you can afford: store-bought products (expensive) or materials from the garden (cheap). Appearance counts, too. For the tidy minded, straw is going to look too messy; for the aesthete, a combination of ground-up leaves and compost will look the most attractive because it creates a consistent dark background for plants.

Ground-up leaves If there's one ideal use for a lawn mower, this is it. You'll need a layer of something on top to hold the leaves in place; manure is fine, but compost is even better. It looks gorgeous, too.

Finely milled bark Don't get those big bark chips; they won't let moisture sink in as effectively and they look awful.

Straw This mulch has a hollow core, which makes it a good insulator. A couple of bales will do for a small garden. Spread the straw around and put a layer of manure or compost on top to keep it from blowing away. It doesn't look very good though.

"Soil is the soul of gardening."

My Ultimate Mulch

My favourite organic mulch is a combination of sheep manure, ground-up leaves and compost with some coir to hold in moisture.

Peat moss mix Though it retains water well, peat is a sterile medium and a lousy mix on its own: if it dries out, it will wick water out of the soil. It must be soaked (split a bale and let the hose dribble onto it overnight) and combined with organic matter. Unfortunately its use is destroying delicate habitats.

Coir mix This is a renewable product made of discarded coconut husks. It holds moisture well, though it must also be moistened and combined with organic material. A mixture of coir, manure and chopped up leaves makes an ideal mulch.

Commercial compost products Bagged composts are good, but expensive to use in quantity. I suggest mixing a bag or two with whatever you have available: leftover potting soil, some topsoil, a few bags of last year's ground-up leaves and good stuff from the compost bin.

Sheet mulching This involves covering an area of grass, weeds or terrible soil with thick layers of newspaper. Wet these down thoroughly so they don't wick moisture out of the soil, top with compost, soil or manure and let sit for a winter if possible. All the material breaks down and you'll end up with amazingly good soil. This is a great way to extend a bed or border without doing a whole lot of work.

Two things are crucial to the success of your garden: your soil and your plants. One does not thrive without care for the other. Soil is the soul of gardening and if you look after it, feed it and protect it, your plants will grow strong and healthy. If a plant does show a problem, you can give it a hit of compost.

The plants in turn will attract beneficial insects and birds into your garden. What you can do for nature pays off with what nature will do for you. With this kind of superb foundation, you know that you can go with confidence to the next step of the process: defining just what you want your garden to be, with the right style and the right plants to suit both you and your site.

Contemporary

Water

Xeriscape

Evening

Evergreen

Formal

Japanese

Contemplative

Set a Garden Style

Informal	Water
Formal	Xeriscape
English Cottage	Evergreen
Japanese	Grass
Contemporary	Evening
Cottage	Contemplative
Country	Rose
Shade	Rock

Set a Garden Style

It's important to set a style for your garden right at the start. This lovely garden capitalizes on a long narrow site by using raised walkways and adapting a calm Japanese style with a modern sensibility in an especially graceful manner. It takes some thought to do it this well and planning is really the key.

JUST AS THERE ARE MANY different types of architectural styles (Georgian, Tudor, contemporary), there are also various garden styles. No matter what size or shape garden you have, any garden style can work in your space. The main determining factors in selecting a style should be the architecture of your house and your own preferences. A large formal garden may not work with a small, seventies, split-level suburban house, but it would be perfect in a neighbourhood full of Georgian or colonial architecture. That said, you also need to consider the kinds of garden that suit your site: shady, full sun, sandy soil and so forth, something that I'll get into later. Your hardiness zone will also have some influence on the style of garden you choose. Putting an English-style garden into a dry, windy site doesn't just look wrong, it feels out of place and untrue to the spirit of the place (the *genius loci*). To define your garden is to mesh the different kinds of garden you can have on your site with the overall style of garden you want and, of course, the kind of gardener you are.

You can start to define your style by looking around your house. It is a gold mine of information about who and what you are—from the furniture you collect to the colour of your living room. Look at objects and spaces that make you feel sensual, wonderful, pleased. Gather ideas you like in gardening magazines and books to find a theme that will lead to your personal style. Visit friends' gardens to refine your vision (creative stealing is always valuable).

Think about what structures and accessories you like (Victorian gazebo, modernist planters) and what materials you favour. For instance, I use stones and wood throughout my garden, with copper details around the house, echoed in the lighting. If you happen to own one superb object such as a piece of sculpture, you can build your whole garden around it with wonderful results. Consider what colours define you best, bearing in mind that hot hues work best in sunny gardens, a cooler palette in shade. Paint colours inside and outside the house should harmonize with plant colours. If you hate anything about either, this is the chance to change them. I found that my garden renovation changed my colour sense so drastically I ended up renovating inside as well as out.

Top left: This simple garden illustrates two good lawn alternatives: *Sagina subulata* (Irish moss) and *S. s.* 'Aurea' (Scotch moss). Despite their names, they are not mosses but look just as good.
Bottom left: A field of glorious lavender has the added benefit of giving off a subtle scent. To keep the rows neat, just cut back to the first signs of growth in the spring.

Another important decision to make as you are defining your garden style is how much lawn you want to keep or get rid of. A lawn can afford cool green respite for the eye amid complex and colourful borders; it can also be a major focal point, a play area for the kids, a place for a dog to run, or a large-scale backdrop for structures and plantings. But lawns figure much less prominently in garden design today compared with the suburban ideal of the fifties when huge sweeps of grass were mandatory. Today's smaller urban gardens can do without a lawn. There are any number of aesthetic alternatives for grass including ornamental grasses, a tapestry of ground covers such as thyme, sweet woodruff and Siberian barren strawberry, or a mix of plants and stones. If you really want to keep some lawn, I recommend keeping it as small as possible and combining it with one of those alternatives.

Among the reasons NOT to have a lawn are: It is a dull and silent place, no butterflies use it, and few beneficial insects inhabit it. Most grasses in lawn seed mixes are not native to North America. Unless you are willing to let them go dormant (and brown) in summer, lawns gobble up huge amounts of water, putting pressure on a precious resource. Finally, weeding and feeding grass takes time, and the temptation to use chemicals to keep it looking putting-green perfect is strong.

Garden Styles

To garden is to extend your house, because that's essentially what a garden is about—living. Ask yourself how you will use the garden: for meditation, for entertaining, as a play space for children, or as a place for the dogs to run? Then decide on your priorities. Be realistic about how much time you will devote to your garden. Some styles, such as formal and Japanese gardens, demand more time and money. Realize, too, that different garden styles involve varying amounts of hardscaping in a wide range of prices; a contemporary walkway of square-cut bluestone pavers will be much more expensive than an informal gravel or bark-chip path. Hardscaping can account for up to 70 percent of a garden's cost, so be sensible about what you can afford to build or buy.

When developing your personal gardening style, remember you aren't just filling up space. Think about what you'd really like to be surrounded by. Get past the ordinary and uninspired; don't feel you have to settle for safe plants: the pine (or rhododendron or clump of pampas grass) stuck in the middle of the lawn, the unbroken swaths of

geraniums, or the single shrub surrounded by impatiens. There are many options to choose from, so start thinking about the styles below to figure out what will work best for you.

As you consider the possibilities, realize that you can create more than one kind of garden within your property. For instance, you might have a contemplative or shade garden in the back under a large tree and a grass garden in an area where there is lots of sun. Whatever kinds of garden you have, however, there should be a consistent style to them. Don't create a Japanese sanctuary in one corner, then plunk a three-tiered Victorian fountain nearby. It's the overall style that will create a vision, and the architecture should be harmonious throughout the garden.

Informal

An informal garden has an underpinning of good design but the edges are curvy and soft, the mood relaxed. Pathways of stone, gravel or brick meander through diverse, flowing plantings. Fences are usually made of wood, furnishings are comfy casual, and a focal point is more likely to be a twig arbour than a Greek goddess. An informal garden still requires regular weeding, watering, deadheading and mulching to look good. This kind of garden suits weekend retreats, family gardens and a house that doesn't have a lot of distinctive architectural features. One of the most famous informal gardens is Vita Sackville-West's white garden at Sissinghurst Castle in England; it is filled with carefully selected plants exuberantly flowing one into another.

Formal

Designed on crisp, straight lines with great symmetry, formal gardens are generally divided into sections or outdoor "rooms." Each one feels self-enclosed, like a room in a house, and is devoted to a particular activity such as dining or sitting. If you have a tidy mind (or a Georgian house), this is the garden style for you. Each area is clearly defined by hedges or walls, which can be high or low depending on the site and the scale of the garden. Paths are smooth and straight, set with square-cut pavers. A fountain, classical sculpture and large urns (in pairs, of course) would also be part of this garden. Such a garden requires a fairly high level of maintenance to keep its meticulous appearance. No dead blooms, no ragged pruning cuts here. Hedges must be sheared on a regular basis; edges kept crisp and neat; and plants trimmed to stay in bounds. Many of the great English gardens with their long walks, symmetrical axes, clipped hedges and giant stone containers embody this style beautifully.

English Cottage

You see this sort of garden gracing thatched cottages on English calendars. It is an amazing rough-and-tumble mix of colourful herbs, vegetables, annuals and perennials, usually herbaceous (which means they disappear in winter). This style of garden depends more on plants that seed themselves and has less infrastructure than the informal garden style. Weathered wood and stone, old bricks and quaint details are the order of the day. Many North American gardeners are seduced by the

"Restraint is key here— nothing is wasted in a Japanese Garden."

Far right: A Japanese garden is not easy to achieve and a Zen garden can seldom be created without professional help. Every element has a symbolic meaning and must relate to every other element in a logical fashion. Many people think this is an excuse for low maintenance. That's just not true. The upkeep on gravel is about the same as the weekly mowing of the lawn.

look of English cottage style only to see it fall flat because it doesn't pair well with our brick-and-aluminum domestic architecture, or because it lacks the structure and winter interest that woody plants provide and that our climate demands. English cottage style has a lively sense of freedom and informality though, and you can still capture that feeling with dynamically mixed borders that incorporate a framework of trees and shrubs. This style of garden is deceptively carefree-looking. In fact, it is well-organized chaos that takes a subtle but firm hand to keep in check. For examples of English cottage style, look to the work of famous English plantswoman and designer Gertrude Jekyll who reinvented this style of gardening in the early twentieth century.

Japanese

The most famous Japanese gardens are found in Kyoto, Japan. Although gardens of this style look simple they are anything but. If you think you might want to build a Japanese garden, do a lot of research. Restraint is key here—nothing is wasted in a Japanese garden. Each rock and each plant has meaning and must be placed just so. To get a Japanese garden right, you will likely need the help of a knowledgeable designer with experience in Japan. If you simply want the feel of a Japanese garden, you can do so with careful use of rocks, a limited plant palette that includes bamboo, and a few meticulously placed objects such as lanterns and screens. Spend the time to build this style of garden well; it takes a good eye, relentless editing and someone willing to learn the intricacies of pruning (or to pay for regular professional pruning). It also takes constant attention to detail: any weed or broken branch will be a glaring oversight. For a fine example of a Japanese garden, visit the Nitobe Memorial Garden in Vancouver, British Columbia.

Contemporary

For the minimalist who loves modern architecture, or has a sleek urban terrace, this style of garden is *de rigueur*. It features clean-lined planters and furniture, edgy accessories and sculptural plants in sophisticated combinations: grasses planted in geometric patterns, a single specimen

Japanese maple, or neat rectangles of ground covers. Form and simplicity rule. Because this garden style demands precise measurements and very clean lines, it is helpful to have a landscape architect or designer create a plan for your space. Contemporary style gardens are usually designed to be low maintenance. Materials such as stone, pebbles, brick and metal require little work except a good hosing down to keep them looking sparkly. Since the designs feature a few select plants, they are fairly simple to water, weed and keep healthy. Gardens designed by American landscape architect Thomas Church or Canada's Janet Rosenberg are good examples of this style.

The following types of gardens are more specific to the site, the purpose or the growing conditions.

Cottage

A garden at the cabin, the cottage or the weekend/holiday retreat has one major principle: it should have no lawn. A lawn intrudes on natural ecosystems, and the work involved maintaining it (along with noise and potential pollution) makes no sense at all. Meadows are more compatible with cottages, perhaps with mown paths through them. (These paths are mowed only a couple of times a summer.) Cottage gardeners should take their cue from the local ecology, and use plants that grow naturally in the area to create integrated and low-maintenance landscapes. (See appendix, page 169, for some great native plants.)

Country

A big country garden should capitalize on its surrounding views and should frame them with mass plantings called drifts (large quantities of the same plant used in a broad sweep). Expansive plantings of things such as Russian sage (*Perovskia*) and coneflowers (*Echinacea* spp.) blur the line between the garden and the surrounding landscape. Structures and plants can be huge and very dramatic (no teensy beds here). Given the scale of this type of property, the plants should be unfussy and easy-care. Hardy, pest-resistant and drought-tolerant ornamental grasses, ferns and lots of native plants work well. For a hit of colour in a sunny spot, you could plant a cutting garden to provide flowers all summer long. (See appendix, pages 165 and 169, for large plants, ornamental grasses and native plants.)

Shade

If your garden space gets little sunlight, consider this a blessing not a curse. A shade garden is one of soft hues and cool abstraction—in other words, a restful garden. Depending on the degree of shade and moisture, a shade garden can be a woodland area filled with native plants, a dappled retreat alight with coloured foliage, or a grotto dripping with greenery. (See appendix, page 168, for a selection of splendid shade plants.)

Water

Water belongs in every garden, even if it is just a small pump bubbling in a tray of stones. But if you have a natural pond or space to build one from scratch, water gardening is a fascinating world to explore. With plants growing underwater, on the water, and by the water, a pond creates a unique ecosystem that attracts a lively mix of insects, birds and other wildlife. In more formal designs, the pond may be a plantless reflecting pond, but still appealing with its straight edges and mirror-like images of the sky.

One concern people have regarding water in the garden is the prevalence of West Nile virus. Mosquitoes feed on the birds that are the carriers for the disease; then they bite humans. Protect yourself by using a good natural insect repellent. Mosquitoes breed in standing water so don't leave any trays, bags or pots lying around where puddles can collect, and change the water in birdbaths every couple of days. A few goldfish in your pond will gobble up any mosquito larvae, and as long as the water is moving in a fountain or bubbler, there won't be a problem.

Water is a necessity in most gardens. It can be a virtue as well, from a container with a self-circulating pump to something more elaborate like this amazing pond. The floor of the pond has been made even more decorative with a lovely checkerboard pattern, and great plants such as hostas and papyrus.

"An evergreen garden needs careful planning to prevent ghastly errors."

Xeriscape

From the Greek word *xeros* meaning "dry," xeriscape means literally "dry landscape." Ideal for hot sunny areas prone to drought, xeriscaping is a way of gardening that combines plants with similar low-watering needs. Native plants, cacti (*Opuntia*), many evergreens, aromatic herbs such as lavender, and succulent plants such as sedums, all find a place in this low-maintenance garden. Water-guzzling lawns do not. This may be the garden of the future as we become more conscious of water conservation.

Evergreen

A garden concentrated on evergreens looks good almost immediately after it is planted and it is the closest thing to a no-maintenance garden. An evergreen garden needs careful planning to prevent ghastly errors like planting a cute little blue spruce that will overwhelm the entire house in about fifteen years. Clever integration of other woody and perennial plants will keep a conifer garden from looking too static. But the huge range of evergreens available in a multitude of sizes and shapes in green, ever-yellow, ever-blue and even variegated forms offers beauty and colour year round. (See appendix, page 164, for some choice conifers.)

Grass

Ornamental grasses make superb specimen plants, elegant hedges and dramatic drifts when massed. Any sunny area would suit a harmonious blend of grasses in various colours, sizes and forms; and there are some shade-tolerant ones, too, such as sedges and Japanese forest grass. Grasses have a brief downtime in spring, look pretty good in summer, and are magnificent in autumn and winter. Easy to maintain, they are excellent problem-solvers in gardens of every size, providing privacy without cutting off views and offering plenty of drama without taking up much space.

If you want a prairie garden, look for prairie grasses such as little bluestem and sideoats grama and mix them with prairie plants such as coneflowers and black-eyed Susans. (See appendix, page 165, for ornamental grasses of all sizes and colours.)

Far right: Evergreens, including yews and boxwood, are worked into a formal, classical setting.

A contemplative garden
always has a retreat like this
enchanting little hut-like
structure. It would fulfill
almost anyone's need to
escape from a hectic life.
The structure also serves as
an outdoor dining room and
is the perfect place to sit
and listen to a soft summer
rain, to think or to meditate.

Evening

Designed to have maximum impact late in the day, the evening garden is
full of white flowers that gleam brightly and are often most fragrant at
night to attract pollinating moths. In supporting roles are silver- and grey-
foliaged plants that reflect light from millions of tiny hairs on their leaves.
Glimmering lanterns, fairy lights, metallic finishes and mirrors bring a
touch of sparkle, while a waterfall or reflecting pond adds to the evening
enchantment. As lovely as this sounds, a romantic moonlit garden doesn't
allow for dead blossoms and demands regular deadheading and grooming.
This is a garden for perfectionists. (See appendix, page 163, for the best
plants with white flowers.)

Contemplative

Pretty much every garden is a healing garden in the sense that being in a
natural setting full of lush greenery is demonstrably beneficial. But for a
contemplative space there should be an aura of calm in both the plants and
the structures. Generally, there will be a path leading to a secret enclosed
spot for sitting amid the plants (this could be a small gazebo swathed in
vines, or a more formal stone arbour). There is texture, fragrance and
always water somewhere, trickling, falling or reflecting. It is a garden of
subtle details and sensory delight, which, of course, should be in every
garden. (See step 5, page 115, for selecting appropriate plants.)

Rose Gardens and Rock Gardens

Two types of gardens that you might dream of—rose gardens and rock
gardens—are challenging even for experienced gardeners. Both are
specialty projects with fussy plants requiring very specific conditions
and a lot of patience. My advice is to integrate roses in a border to get a
rose hit, and learn how to handle them one species at a time, starting
with tough rugosa roses. To enter the world of rock gardens, I suggest
you join a rock garden group (the North American Rock Garden Society
has chapters across the country) and learn before you leap into this
fascinating type of gardening.

Having worked through the pregardening process and explored the
various garden styles, you should have a good sense of what your site is
all about and what kind of garden will reflect you and your personal
style. This part of the process can take up to a year, but using that time
to define an overall style for a rich and diverse garden is crucial.

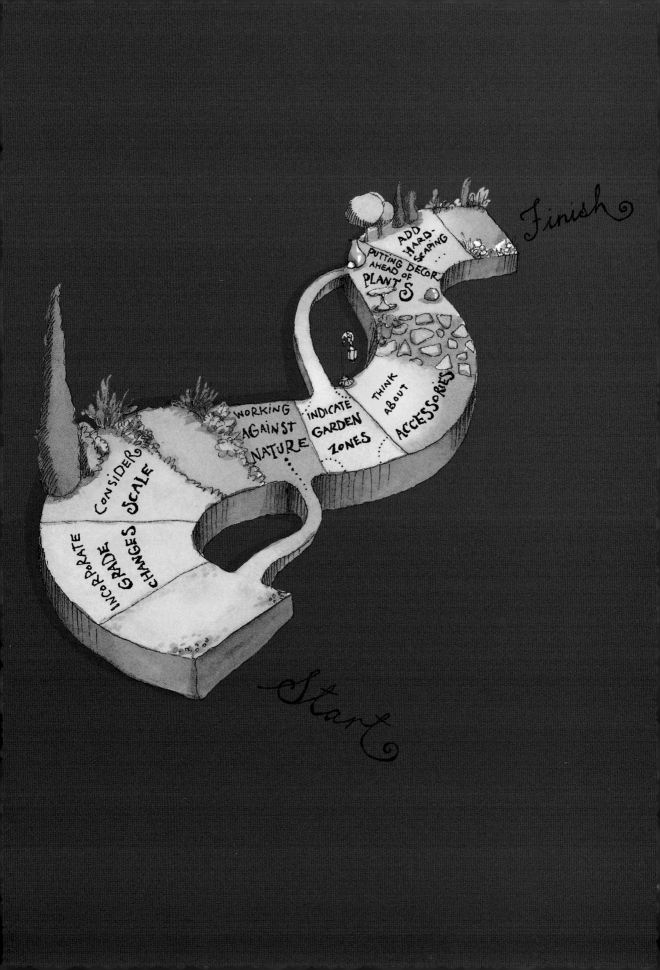

Make a Garden Map

How to Get Started
Drawing Your Garden Map
The Elements of Hardscaping
The Elements of Softscaping

Make a Garden Map

The well-designed garden
has a path, edges that are
well tended and sharp,
distinct levels, areas suited
to your needs and a good
variety of plants.

NOW IT'S TIME TO MAKE A GARDEN MAP to get a sense of what features your space can accommodate, and to decide on the overall layout. A map will also help you figure out your priorities and what you want to tackle first. It's often easier to install a garden one section at a time than implement the entire thing in one fell swoop. When designing a garden, you are dealing with so many issues (light, the seasons, the site, your own needs and wishes) that it's hard to keep everything straight in your head. A garden map helps and all it requires is a piece of paper and a pen—and maybe a glass of wine.

Part of this exercise involves trying to fit in all the things you want in your garden. But you'll probably have more stuff in the garden of your dreams than your budget or space will allow, and it's easier to remove things on paper than on the ground. Our map on page 68 has far too much in it—it's simply a guide to all the things you could conceivably include. A garden can't have everything, but it must have those wonderful things that will make you happy and comfortable.

How to Get Started

Take pictures from every room in the house overlooking the garden—they will help you focus on what should go where. Make a list of everything you'd like to see in your new garden, things such as an arbour, a herb garden, a fountain or fruit trees. Then cut the list in half. Simplify, simplify. It's better to have one gorgeous piece of sculpture than a mess of garden gargoyles. Think of a garden as a stage set where every element has a reason to be on stage.

Don't forget the practical items. Think about where to put a composter (preferably out of sight), a garden shed and maybe a potting bench/work area. Getting into the garden is often a forgotten factor—through the house is not a good idea (especially when it comes to lugging large muddy pots of plants). Decide how to provide access from the house or through a side yard, how to move people through the garden, and how to reach the shed, the composter or work area. Where will the paths be placed? Paths are the skeleton of a garden; get them right early on and you will have a great underpinning for your design.

Starting Notes

A garden begins in your head. Think about what you need the garden for, what you want the place to look like. Just following a few simple guidelines and making sure you avoid my garden sins will make a huge difference to the results you get and to your budget. It's a garden fact: you can't have everything but you can certainly try.

Before you put pencil to paper, there are some special elements and design principles to keep in mind during the garden-planning process. I've listed my ten pet peeves for garden designing below; this chapter will show you how to avoid committing these garden sins:

1. Working against nature; for example, planting sun-loving plants in the shade or exposing shade-lovers to the sun where they will be scorched.
2. Buying one of everything you see at the nursery. Doing this without a planting scheme in mind will result in a design mishmash with no sense of style.
3. Having too many different hardscaping elements. This can end up looking fragmented and confused. One big rock is better than a truckload of little ones; one wide stone path is better than three narrow ones of gravel, bark chips and pavers.
4. Putting decor ahead of the most important part of the garden—the plants. Keep the tchotchkes to a minimum the first year, then acquire them one piece at a time.
5. Jamming in too many plants in an area for instant effect. This might work for some small perennials but you can't do it with trees and shrubs; they will languish. Annuals are better for filling up spaces.
6. Installing plants without accounting for their ultimate size. That tiny stick of a blue spruce will reach 100 feet (30 metres) eventually, so never plant something like that too close to the house.
7. Planting a shrub or tree smack dab in the middle of the lawn and expecting elegance. This condemns the plant to a life of competition with the grass for water and nutrients—definitely not a healthy situation.
8. Forgetting to plant one great native tree and some structural shrubs before anything else.
9. Waiting too long to plant vines. These are the walls, the wallpaper, even the paint of the garden room. They should be installed at the outset.
10. Not having a composter. You will get use out of even a small one, and it will change your mind about how effective organic gardening is.

Grade Changes

A flat site is easier to work on, but variations in level make for a more interesting garden, even if they are confined to a single raised planting

Raised beds make a really big difference to the microclimate in any given area of a garden. A bed raised with stones and back filled with good garden soil will perform incredibly well. Here Shasta daisies and coreopsis run together in a lavish display. This kind of bed will break out in bloom during the earliest part of spring, so it's wise to load it up with bulbs.

bed. So as you walk about your garden, look for existing features to enhance or for opportunities to add dimension. Make depressions deeper, rises higher, but make them generous, not saucers or pimples. You can contour a flat site by making a berm, a long substantial mound of earth. The berm should be grand—at least 10 feet (3 metres) long and 4 feet (1.2 metres) high. Build it by throwing all the biodegradable garden detritus in a pile and covering it with a good triple mix (a combination of compost, topsoil and sand). Voila, a planting bed par excellence. A really steep slope may require terracing and, to be safe, this demands professional help. If that can't be done right away, plant the slope with ground covers such as barren strawberry or daylilies to hold the soil in place. If you can't physically change your flat site, you can still achieve the appearance of levels by using plants of varying heights when the time comes.

Enclosure

Enclosure (of all or part of a garden) is an important aspect of any good design. The space should be a serene but animated retreat from the world outside. Assess the degree and quality of enclosure you have already; what can be kept (an existing hedge, for example) and where it needs improvement (cover a stretch of chain-link fence with vines, or replace it altogether). Enclosure doesn't take a high stone wall, though that would be nice. It's more likely to be a solid fence (usually wood but possibly metal, bamboo or Plexiglas), something not to be taken lightly. You'll build two fences in your garden's life: the very first one you decide on and the second one that will go in when you are revamping the

"Gardening is about visual literacy, and that comes with understanding scale."

garden in fifteen years. Fences can also enhance a garden's perspective: horizontal lengths of lathing will emphasize a narrow garden's depth, for instance. If you have a potential vista, think of how you keep it while maintaining an enclosed feeling. You can cut out parts of the fence to provide glimpses of the view; use trees and shrubs to frame the view; or set up a mirror to reflect the view while you are ensconced amid your own greenery.

Scale

Gardening is about visual literacy, and that comes with understanding scale. This is the relationship between objects: how big or how small they are and how they relate to each other. Scale is crucial: when something in the garden is too big, it feels overwhelming; if it's too small, it looks insignificant. Garden design is made more difficult because there are two forces no other art form except architecture has to deal with—the sky and the horizon.

You may realize that the new sofa is too big once it's in your living room, but did you have this feeling in the showroom? Probably not. Outdoors, *everything* seems smaller. You have to scale up what you think is the right size because the natural tendency is to make things such as a patio or a border too small. Conversely, we often underestimate the size plants will grow to and can end up with a giant tree throwing everything out of whack.

It's important to get the garden features in the right scale at the beginning. If you make your pond too small, you will be changing it down the road; the same applies to a patio. The features should also relate to each other in scale for proper balance (just like getting that sofa to work with the armchair and coffee table). To get a sense of the right scale of things you'll be putting on your map, try the following: Wherever you decide to have a structure, a large tree or a shrub, go to that spot in the garden and pile up boxes—or even make a replica of what you are going to install—to get a sense of the volume. Use bamboo stakes in tepee form to determine size and placement of an obelisk, or run string along a length of bamboo stakes to gauge the proper height of a screen or fence.

Consider acquiring a chalk marker (a gizmo used by construction guys to spray a chalk line) and outlining the proposed major structures, pond or borders so you can study them from every angle and adjust the proportions as needed.

Drawing Your Garden Map

When you start drawing your garden map don't worry if it is very rough and has a lot of extraneous stuff on it. It's where you are working things out. Most of us get bogged down because we want things to be perfect, but your garden map does not need absolute accuracy. Go out into the garden with a measuring tape—or use your site survey—and get the correct proportions for the length and width of the property. Put that basic outline on your map and roughly block in the area the house takes up. Mark in existing structures, large trees and any significant characteristics of the land such as slopes, big rocks or a stream. Then mark in the sunniest and shadiest spots. Draw lines where you know paths are needed, making these crucial links as simple as possible (not too many wiggles) and wide enough to walk along easily (a minimum of 3 feet/90 centimetres). Copy this basic outline about ten times because you'll be making lots of revisions. Begin by following these steps, though you can go back and revise any time.

Delineating Garden Zones

Look at your map and divide up the garden into spaces or pockets according to their specific purposes, such as dining, sitting, playing or swimming. When you do this, you'll find the garden almost naturally divides itself into garden rooms: each space has a function just like the rooms of your house.

Next, draw the axial lines on your map: one straight down the middle, another on the horizontal halfway across, and a third and fourth criss-crossing the centre point on an angle. These lines will help you achieve a balanced placement for specific features. Then, drawing rough blobs, designate the following zones within the garden rooms. Each garden room should have at least two of these three zones:

ZONE A
Entertaining
area

TABLE

BERM

ZONE C

Houses

PERGOLA

ZONE B
FOCAL POINT

ZON

POTS TO
DISGUISE
BBQ

ZONE A
BBQ area

jungle gym

sculpture

A highly theoretical garden map. A real one, based on your own space, is so useful that you should make dozens of copies of your basic plan. Then keep adding layers. No garden would have all of the elements we've chosen to show. It would be too fussy and crowded. Err on the side of simplicity. Use the axiom of: here's what I want, I'll remove two-thirds and here's what I'll get. By dividing the garden up into pockets as suggested here, you can work on one area at a time and not get overwhelmed either physically or financially.

ZONE A – LIVING AREAS The main Zone A area should be placed close to your house; this is where you'll be having dinner alfresco and doing your entertaining. It will no doubt include a deck or a patio—the biggest, most expensive item to be installed. It's also the area that is most visible from the house and planning it well gives instant satisfaction. Then designate Zone A areas in other garden rooms: a dog run, a sandbox, work bench or children's play area or even a croquet lawn.

Sketch in generous spaces for specific features such as furniture in the dining area. Measure the size of your table, as well as your chairs when they are pushed back as far as necessary, so you can calculate how much wiggle room you'll need. Make the space large enough to accommodate a barbecue (well-disguised with screens or big pots of plants), containers with culinary herbs, and at least one comfortable chair for lounging. Since Zone A is right by the house, make it square with the house or the centre of the garden; putting it off-kilter will drive you crazy.

ZONE B – FOCAL POINTS A focal point is an object or feature such as an urn, a statue or arbour visible at a distance. It draws you into the garden and becomes a destination. Line up a focal point with the central axis of the garden at the end of a pathway. You can also place it to one side of the garden, as long as it is balanced on the opposite side with artifacts or plantings. You might want several focal points such as a water feature, a pergola, gazebo, garden shed or other structures. Keep both the material and building style of structures consistent.

ZONE C – PLANTING ZONES Allot Zone C areas according to sun (these are referred to as sun spots), shade, part-sun and part-shade areas. Label them clearly so you will have an idea of what plants to consider for each zone.

Start by marking in at least one big tree if you don't have one already or haven't planted one in the pregardening phase. It can anchor the whole garden. To get it in the right position, use a friend or relative as a stand-in (be sure to get a picture of them looking this ridiculous) and shift them about until the spot where your tree will be placed feels perfect from every vantage point. Make sure the tree and any structures give each other plenty of room (at least 6 feet / 1.8 metres). To enhance the tree's placement, plant at least two shrubs at a sensible distance from the tree taking into account their ultimate widths as listed on the tags. Think of the shrubs as works of art and place them to create a sense of depth and movement.

It's always good to have evergreens: they suit all styles of garden and provide a habitat for birds and roosting spots for butterflies. Try to accommodate existing healthy evergreens or place new ones where they will be visible in winter, which is when they'll shine, and be sure to allow for their ultimate size. I'd suggest a minimum of three evergreens, even in a small garden as long as they are of appropriate dimensions (read those tags).

Slot in borders, making them as large as possible and avoiding complicated shapes. Take it from experience, you'll quickly become dissatisfied with a 2-foot (60-centimetre) border all around the

perimeter of your yard. If the border is more than 10 feet (3 metres) deep, though, you'll need access paths or stepping stones. There is a lot of flexibility here: borders can define a space, edge a structure, surround a tree, follow a path, or simply be an island border in the middle of the lawn. Rough them in on your map; you'll refine them once you start translating the design into reality.

If you have a swimming pool, don't let it become the most important factor of the garden room, with plants as mere add-ons. Put planting zones around the pool but far enough away so the plants won't drop a lot of debris into the water, or be damaged by pool splash. Chlorine won't kill plants immediately but it will if the water is perpetually sloshing over them. Pools are usually fenced, so earmark space along the fence for vines such as clematis or Virginia creeper.

Pick a sunny spot for a vegetable, herb or cutting garden if one or all are desired and draw in spaces for pots of annuals and perennials (see page 84). Finally, if you have children, give them a little place to grow something. A raised bed 2 feet (60 centimetres) square is enough space for them to fill with colourful, easy-to-grow plants such as sunflowers and morning glories.

Divide your garden into different zones or pockets to fulfill each part of your design. Discrete zones can be accomplished, as this smart gardener has done, with interior hedges and walls, walks and benches and by judicious use of planters. These divisions or interior walls give the garden a more complex layered look, making each area a wonderful little surprise unto itself.

Placing Interior Garden Walls

You need to pay special attention to the walls of your garden room or rooms; these interior walls define the individual spaces, provide privacy, hide workaday stuff such as the composter, and offer opportunities for vertical plantings. Yew, laurel or boxwood hedges make gorgeous interior walls but require patience since they take several years to get established. Other options include trellises, wooden screens or even a large plant. Just be careful you don't put too many hard structures in a small garden or things will start to look cluttered.

Interior walls also help to give a garden a sense of mystery. Ideally, you should never be able to take in the whole garden at once. In addition to screens and hedges, you can create allure with such things as a pathway that disappears around a bend, or a gate that affords a peekaboo view. Take your map outside and try to visualize your design to see where a tall ornamental grass or shrub or structure might provide added enticement.

Consider Your Composition

Now that you have all your rooms and zones in place, check to see if your proposed garden has a thought-out composition. Look at the axial line down the centre of your map and make sure all the structures, the borders and the paths on one side are balanced by the components on the other side. The two sides should appear harmonious and feel naturally satisfying. The balance may be symmetrical in that everything on one side is precisely mirrored on the other, or asymmetrical in that there are different components on each side but their forms, size and colour have equal weight. You might have to move things around on your map. This process is a little like understanding the composition of a painting; it will click when you get it right.

What you have done so far is a mind-clearing exercise, determining what belongs on your map and what doesn't. Now comes the critical point: filling in the details of all those blobs. This is the most fun because you'll be seeing your garden finally take shape.

The Elements of Hardscaping

Whatever hardscaping elements you use will become, along with woody plants, the bones of your whole design. These are what show up in winter and, if these components are done properly, your garden will look compelling in every season. Don't worry about being able to afford all

"Bricks won't stand up to huge amounts of traffic but will have a great aesthetic appeal."

the elements of hardscaping immediately. Think about what you would like, a fountain for instance, and put it on your map—that way you'll know there's just the right spot waiting for it. Gardens are for dreaming and you can always use huge containers or big ornamental grasses as a substitute in the meantime.

Paths and Paving

Once you have determined where your generous paths are going, consider what they will be made of. You want a look that will be appropriate to your style of garden, but also think about maneuvering wheelbarrows, heaving bags of leaves, and wrangling hoses along them, and choose your surface material accordingly. Crazy paving that uses irregularly shaped stones is inexpensive because it doesn't involve precise cuts and tight joins. It can easily be set in concrete but has a tendency to move in winter. For a formal or contemporary look, use more expensive square-cut stones. Gravel is another inexpensive pathway material and comes in many sizes, textures and colours. It looks more sophisticated than crazy paving and works in contemporary or informal settings.

Another option to consider is a stepping stone path using limestone squares, often found in a Japanese stroll garden (so called because the spaces between the stones make the walker slow down). It's hell to drag anything along this kind of path but lovely to look at because ultimately the plants fill in the spaces for a tapestry look.

If you find a cache of weathered old bricks, get an artisan to lay them out in an unusual design. Bricks won't stand up to huge amounts of traffic but will have great aesthetic appeal. Alternatively, try raised wooden paths, like a boardwalk through a "pond of plants," or crisply edged grass paths that should be at least 3 feet (90 centimetres) for easy upkeep. For an excellent book on path construction, check out *Garden Paths: Inspiring Designs and Practical Projects* by Gordon Hayward.

Far right, top: The perfect welcoming garden path of gravel, heading toward a focal point at the bridge and into the countryside beyond. The yarrow (*Achillea* spp.) in the foreground will brighten up any scene.
Far right, bottom: The ultimate wooden path, which crosses a pond to a deck-seating area. These paths fit perfectly in the style of each garden, from country to contemporary.

Furnish the garden with the same thought for comfort as you do your living room. This delightful sitting area has all the earmarks of both taste and care: the little starry lights, a mirror which acts like a window with a table set in front of it and two great garden chairs.

Patios and Decks

These are probably the largest, and most expensive, items you'll be putting into your garden so consider their size and scale carefully. How will they relate to both the house and garden, and how much space will you actually need? Because a patio or deck is a long-term investment, choose a terrific design and use the best materials you can afford.

Fences

Before installing a fence around the perimeter of your property, you should know exactly where your property lines are and find out what the local bylaws are regarding height restrictions. Also, ask your neighbours what they want since it is a common feature (and whether they'll pay for half the cost). There are many fence styles ranging from solid privacy fences to open lattice panels in different materials including wood, metal and Plexiglas. Choose a style that complements the architecture of the house and the rest of the garden structures as well as the style that you've chosen for your garden.

Furnishings and Accessories

Furnishing an outdoor room is similar to furnishing an indoor room. Buy good pieces one at a time; don't worry about everything matching, but watch out for clutter. This can happen so easily in the rush to make a comfortable outdoor living room. And make sure what you buy fits the aesthetic you've decided on. For instance, to get that French feeling, look for bistro chairs, small tables or *faux bois* furniture. For a Japanese-influenced garden, look for benches or stools fashioned from cubes of magnificent, recycled old-growth wood.

The well-furnished patio or deck needs a table and chairs to seat four to eight people. For more guests, add tables in different parts of the garden. Make sure they can be moved easily and have comfortable cushions. The array of outdoor fabrics now available is fantastic; it is easy to coordinate cushion colours with the palette you've chosen for the garden and your home's interior. Outdoor table lighting doesn't depend on votive candles any more; now there are battery-driven lamps and fake candles that look great and are weatherproof.

Let your imagination rip when choosing statuary and art. Hide them, tuck them into corners, make one a focal point. Never install a large object permanently until you've left it in place for a few days. But don't leave it too long—it's amazing what the eye will become accustomed to.

Don't forget that well-designed unadorned obelisks can be used like pieces of sculpture. Invest in one great container and choose a plant for it that echoes its shape and complements its colour.

Mirrors can be placed at an angle to make a garden seem wider, or set behind a screen to make it seem deeper. Unfortunately, there is a downside: birds tend to bash into mirrors and some, such as cardinals, will mistake the reflection as an interloper and try to peck it to death. You might have to place shrubs or long pieces of reflective foil in front of the mirrors to discourage them.

Rocks

To my mind, all gardens need rocks or stones in one form or another, whether it is a stone patio, a waterfall, a gravel path, a retaining wall, a rock garden or a single splendid boulder anchoring a planting. Far too many yards, however, look as though a truck has backed up and dumped the local river bottom on the front lawn. That plus a limp evergreen and a couple of annuals equals low-maintenance gardening at its worst. Respected and used properly, rocks not only contribute colour and texture to garden decor, but also give a sense of Canada's amazing geological past.

If possible, use local rock, which is much cheaper because of lower haulage fees. Be sure to plan how much help you will need getting the rocks to where you want them in the garden. Large boulders will require a professional with a backhoe. When setting rocks, large or small, always sink them well into the ground for stability and to give a natural look of permanence. Scale, once again, is critical. Build a mock-up with twigs or cardboard boxes to determine if your planned rock is too large or too

Far left: I love this little
front garden, which has the
perfectly placed rock, sunk
to about one-third its depth
and surrounded by blooms
in three seasons—here irises
and *Phlox subulata*.
Left: A well-lit garden is a
work of art. Night lighting
usually requires the help of
an expert. Spending some
extra time researching
suppliers to find one whose
taste matches yours won't
cost any more, and will
really be more worthwhile.
Lighting is a big investment.

small. Use plants that like the reflected heat from rocks and the cool
moist root run they afford such as irises, alpine plants, grasses and bulbs.

Water Features

Water is wonderful in a garden; it brings sound, movement and all sorts
of wildlife. Today you can buy almost any form of water feature, from
ponds and waterfalls to fountains and Japanese stone basins, at a large
nursery or water gardening specialist. You must have some skill at
installing these things before taking one on, and very elaborate systems
will probably require expert help. Whatever type of water feature you
choose, it should fit in with the style of your garden and also be in scale.
Waterfalls can be stunning but require carefully placed stones to create
a natural flow as well as a pleasing composition.

Lighting

Consider lighting and the installation of outdoor wiring at the start
of the design process and you will save time and money and achieve
an improved design. So much of our garden living takes place in the
evening, and the transformative quality of extraordinary lighting can
make it an exhilarating time.

LIGHTING TERMS

Uplighting is a light shining upward, usually onto a focal point or a
specimen tree. The fixture can be on or in the ground. Be picky about
the trees you decide to illuminate—if you have too much lighting, you
highlight nothing.
Downlighting involves placing lights high in a tree or on a structure.
It is very dramatic and, with the right combination of fixtures, can look
like moonlight.
Backlighting places a light behind an object so it is silhouetted in the
beam. It works beautifully with shapely trees or grasses.
Shroud or hood is essentially the lamp's shade. There are many different
styles, from a mushroom cap or a tulip to a Chinese hat.

TYPES OF LIGHTS

Solar lights: Running off the power of the sun, these lights need no
wiring. But forget about using them in a shady yard.
Low voltage lights: These give maximum light with little electricity. They
require transformers to convert household current to the lower voltage.

Light Magic

Lights are a great way to get the best out of your garden. They will disguise a very young garden and enhance one that's more mature. Don't over light; add enough to make pathways safe if you use them at night. Be mysterious: a little light highlighting an old tree can add enchantment.

LEDs: Light-emitting diodes (like the indicator lights on audio-visual equipment) are long-lasting, low-power, cool-burning lights usually used to illuminate walkways. Available in different colours, they are being employed in various ways, including as Christmas tree lights and inside garden umbrellas.

HIDs: High intensity discharge lights such as metal halide are very bright, have a long life, and use less power than incandescent lights. Often used in indoor hydroponic gardening, they make fine outdoor floodlights and are ideal to illuminate big trees.

Fibre optics: Light from a single source travels through filaments of glass or plastic to create some dazzling effects. Relatively expensive but very versatile, these lights can illuminate pools underwater, outline structures, festoon trees or be tucked between deck boards to create a carpet of stars.

Although there are plenty of DIY lighting kits at the hardware stores, this is one area it's worth getting expert advice about from a lighting designer. Lighting isn't just decorative. At a minimum, you need lights for security and safety: stairs, alleys, side yards, dark hedging and paths (especially if they are on a steep incline and have an uneven surface). Once those lights are in place, you can start getting fancy. You'll also need to gauge how much light is already emanating from the windows of the house, the neighbours' and street lights. Street lights tend to overpower anything you can possibly add. Be courteous and never beam light into a neighbour's garden.

On a practical level, keep any wires susceptible to damage by raccoons and squirrels out of trees, and always ask these questions: How resistant is any lighting unit to water and to UV rays? Can you change the bulbs easily or is an expert required?

Aging the Garden

Giving the garden a settled look of solidity and age is an important rule of good garden design. It takes away that newly planted rawness. Garden collectibles are an easy way of achieving an established look. They may be architectural remnants (decorative grates, stone finials) or any object that has some relevance to horticulture (old watering cans or pots, even bits of ancient farm machinery). But there is a danger of becoming obsessed by them. A collection should lend character to a new garden but never overwhelm it. If the objects of your desire are too obvious, start

Clockwise from top left: A statue, like this one, looks perfectly at home guarding her well-placed plants; use old artifacts like this old-fashioned corbel to give an aged feel to your space; an armillary sphere adds age and grace to a garden.

Borders or planting beds can bracket a garden, or describe sensuous curves as they do in this splendid garden. Borders should always have well-defined edges—or use plants that become edgers—to announce a full planting area. To keep edges crisp use a border spade with a flat edge on a regular basis.

taking them out one at a time. Group items together gracefully and think of ways to create surprise displays: a shelf full of old pots or ancient watering cans hung on a fence. Make sure there's a place for everything before you buy (this falls on deaf ears, of course, if you are a serious collector). Always remember plants first, collectibles second.

In addition, you can try the following aging techniques:

- Enhance any established trees by having them properly pruned, and use weathered-looking finishes of silvery grey on fences and screens.
- Prowl your neighbourhood to find old bricks and bits of grillwork that can be placed around the garden.
- Save broken vases and large containers—shoved into the ground, they take on a whole new life.
- Paint a mixture of beer and water, or just plain acidophilus yogurt, on stones. Keep them moist and moss will grow, making them look as though they have been there forever.
- Look for a chair or plinth with a few chips and peeling paint, and stick it in a border as if it were a forgotten monument.
- Give containers a sense of history by painting them soft grey, white, or black and earth tones then let them chip and flake, even split. Indoor paint used outside will break down quickly.

WITH THE HARDSCAPING SLOTTED in on your map, you can work out the best location for the barbeque gas line and where you will need electrical outlets. If you decide to get an irrigation system, the installer will lay it out, but it will have to be coordinated with your plantings to be effective.

The Elements of Softscaping

When gardeners refer to softscaping they are talking about plants. Just as in hardscaping, softscaping involves many choices, but making these decisions is the raison d'être and real joy of gardening. Yes, you can have a garden that is all hardscape and hard edges. But to my mind that is incredibly boring and lifeless. Plants are what it's all about. Before deciding on specific plants, though, it's important to understand how plants create and complement your design.

At this point, you should have your map with the major hardscaping elements, a big tree (or trees) with a couple of companion shrubs and some evergreens sketched in. Now it's time to decide where you need screening plants: these are tall shrubs that will blot out anything you don't want to see, such as an ugly garage or the composter. You might need a whole row of screening plants or only one here and there, but get them in place. Mark in any lawn areas and also allot space for any hedges that will form the interior walls of your garden room or rooms. Next, and this is the most fun, you can start to figure out how you are going to fill in those blobs designated as planting zones or borders.

When you actually start implementing the borders you've drawn on your map, you will need to refine their shape and size. First, go out into your garden and outline each proposed border with a hose, string or chalk marker, keeping the shape simple. Check what it looks like from where it will be viewed, especially from indoors, and adjust the shape and size. Trust me, you'll probably want to double it.

Borders can be all shrubs, all perennials or even all annuals. But my preference is for a mixed border consisting of graduated layers of plants going from small trees and shrubs, to a dynamic combination of perennials and annuals, right down to tiny ground covers, with bulbs interwoven throughout to create a richly textured, ever-changing tapestry. This much structure will make a border look good all year round and is easy to add to as your taste changes. Borders can mirror each other (have the same plantings) or echo each other (similar colours but different species).

Specimen and Anchor Plants

Start with a great shrub or small tree as a focal point; this is usually called a specimen plant and will be large enough to mark on the map. It has to be something dramatic and shapely, and can go in the centre or off to one side depending on how symmetrical a design you want. Be sure to mark it on the map—they take up a fairly large volume of space. In my garden, I have the Eastern redbud cultivar 'Forest Pansy'; it has large purple leaves that are especially ravishing when backlit by the morning sun.

Secondly, you need anchor plants. Smaller than the specimen plant, these are standout plants in terms of size, colour and texture used to punctuate and lend substance to the space. They also act as foils to the plants beside them. Anchor plants can be woody plants, ornamental grasses or architectural perennials such as giant mullein (*Verbascum*) or bear's breeches (*Acanthus*). The classic way to use them is by placing them at each end of a border like bookends, but these days designers are setting them in the middle and clustering other plants around them for a more complex effect.

The Middle Layer

Surrounding the anchor plants will be a mix of perennials and perhaps smaller shrubs. Consider using some dwarf evergreens such as low-growing junipers and pines because they offer unvarying form and colour amid a constantly changing array.

Fillers, Edgers and Carpets

Because perennials take at least two years to reach their mature size, you can fill in any blank spaces with annuals. Some useful filler plants, such as forget-me-nots and golden feverfew, don't need to be planted afresh every year since they will seed themselves about the garden. Edgers are low-growing plants such as coral bells, blue fescue and small hostas used along the edge of a border or walkway. Using strong edgers in consistent tones and texture will add just the right fillip of colour and define the shape of the border. Carpeting plants are the low ground-covering plants such as Siberian barren strawberry and golden creeping Jenny that you can tuck around trees and shrubs and in any spots that won't accommodate larger plants.

Scale, Texture and Form

As you work on your planting designs, remember to keep the plants in scale with the garden and each other. It might be an intriguing notion to have a garden of nothing but huge plants, but they would become overbearing. The ideal is a garden with variations of height, shape, colour and especially texture. All plants have multiple textures. For instance, a

Far right: The most amazing gardens, like this one, will always be created in layers. Daylilies, coreopsis, thymes, globe thistle and spreading junipers flourish in the foreground. The pink plants are *Saponaria officinalis*, which is a spreader and should only be used where there's plenty of space. Borders can also be islands of plantings placed anywhere in the garden.

shrub may have very dense, twiggy growth or a very open branching pattern so the overall texture is either opaque or light. In addition, its leaves may be large or small (creating another overall texture) and the leaves themselves may be smooth or puckered, silky or bristly (yet another texture). Shrubs with dense textures obviously make good screens while those with open textures can be used like a theatrical scrim; I strategically place shrubs such as the 'Diabolo' ninebark to partly conceal the garden and partly draw the eye into it. An effective border has a contrast of foliage sizes and textures.

In addition, look for contrast in the plant forms: upright spikes (irises) against rounded mounds (hardy geraniums); tall cylindrical shapes (delphiniums) against wide spreading ones (peonies). There's a lot to take into account when designing your borders, but that is all part of gardening's endless fascination.

Designing with Containers

Containers are pots or planter boxes with drainage holes in the bottom. They should be as large as possible and of as fine a quality as possible because every garden needs containers if only to fill in empty spaces in

Containers are a garden's best asset. They can be set out with one plant per pot, as in this elegant arrangement of *Echeveria* spp.—one of the very best plants to use in a container, especially on a windy balcony. Indeed, a collection of containers can be shown off with or without plants.

borders during the dog days of summer. However, used badly they just clutter up the joint and look awful. If in doubt, use one huge container as a focal point—get a very modern metal or fibreglass one that will withstand freezing—and change the planting with every season.

Containers should relate to the style of the garden, the house and each other. You can plant them with annuals that will provide instant bloom or with perennials that take a couple of years to show their stuff. You can design a whole garden with containers, of course, but experiment with them in clever ways so they add height, bulk or a jolt of surprise. For example, try setting a bunch of pots on a step ladder or plinth in a border to create a layered effect. No matter what you do, when designing with containers remember the following tips.

1. Use containers in transitional areas (porches, doorways, entry courtyards) to continue colours from house to garden.
2. Move large containers around while they are empty to get them in the right spot. Once filled, these things weigh a ton.
3. Make sure any container is raised off the ground on bricks or chocks to aid drainage and to keep them from freezing and cracking in winter.
4. Put poolside containers on casters so they can be easily moved out of the sun—the heat reflection from the water can be brutal—or out of the way at pool-party time.
5. To make a garden appear longer, place large containers in the foreground and set increasingly smaller ones behind.
6. Avoid using silly, little containers. Buy larger ones than you think you'll need; little pots dotted about look haphazard and uncomfortable.
7. Match the pot to the plant's ultimate size. Don't place a small plant in a huge container or vice versa.
8. Never put big containers on pedestals. It is unsafe and unnecessary.
9. Make sure containers sit absolutely level. It is visually insulting to see containers listing sideways.
10. Use a gravel mulch in containers to hold in moisture and discourage squirrels.

Designing a garden on paper will help you make major decisions about what to install, what you can afford immediately and how much work you are prepared to invest in your new garden. You don't have to follow your garden map slavishly but at least you will have some ideas firmly in place when you begin to select plants, which is what you want to do next.

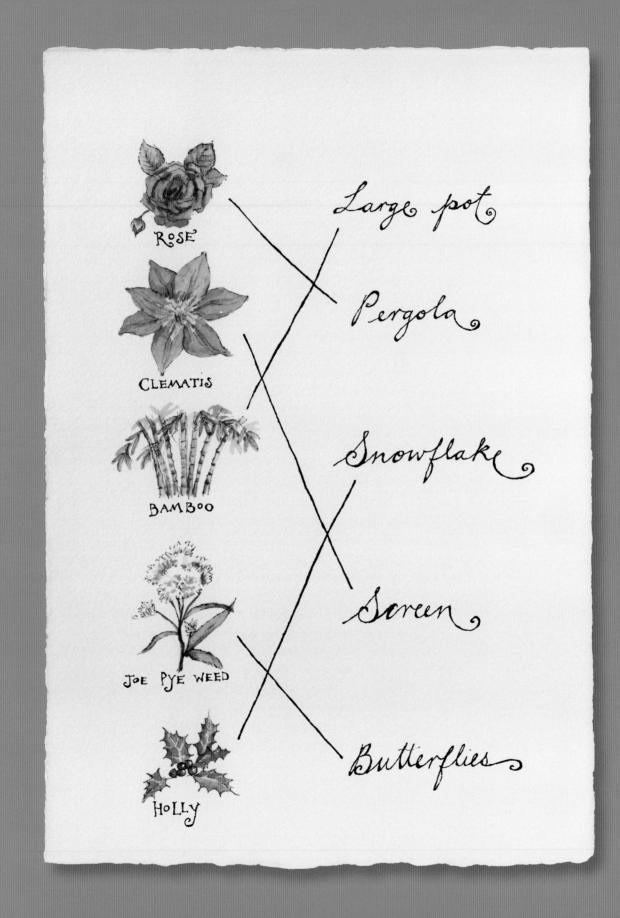

ROSE

CLEMATIS

BAMBOO

JOE PYE WEED

HOLLY

Large pot

Pergola

Snowflake

Screen

Butterflies

How to Select Plants

Shopping
For Colour
Trees and Shrubs
Vines
Ornamental
Grasses
Ground Covers
Annuals
Herbs
Bulbs

For Containers
For Shade
Native Plants
For Contemplative
Gardens
For Autumn
Colour
For Winter
Interest

How to Select Plants

This glorious garden has a mix of perennials including herbs, unusual bulbs such as alliums and a combination of great small and large trees. It shows how well thinking in layers serves a gardener.

NOW THAT YOUR DESIGN IDEAS ARE ON PAPER, the fun part begins. Selecting, moving, dividing and playing with plants is what brings out the creative juices. It stretches you intellectually and physically. Combinations of plants are thrilling: one bloom echoing the colour in another, two foliage plants blending one into another, companions that will dazzle for years. This is the essence of gardening.

All inspired gardens are a mix of plants—trees, shrubs, vines, perennials, annuals, bulbs—not only for year-round beauty but also for their diversity. The greater the variety of plants, the greater the number of birds, bugs and micro-organisms, resulting in a healthier garden less prone to pests and diseases. This variety and complexity of life is called biodiversity.

Zones and Microclimates

It's a good idea to find out what plant hardiness zone you live in, so you will know what plants you can grow easily. Nurseries generally sell trees, shrubs and perennials that are hardy locally, but it's wise to know your zone when you are doing your research so you don't get your heart set on something inappropriate. A plant's zone number is an indication of its hardiness—its ability to survive certain conditions. Canada is divided into nine plant hardiness zones based largely on average minimum temperatures, Zone 0 being the coldest and Zone 8 the warmest. So a plant marked Zone 4 will survive in that zone and warmer; in colder zones, it will die. Of course, just to complicate things, the United States has eleven zones. It means that a plant labelled Zone 5 in the United States would be Zone 6 in Canada (no one said this would be easy). Both the Canadian and US governments have websites where you can find out what hardiness zone you are in:

- Canada: http://sis.agr.gc.ca/cansis/nsdb/climate/hardiness
- United States: www.usna.usda.gov/Hardzone/ushzmap.html

It's very helpful to know your zone so that you can avoid buying plants that aren't hardy and thus doom them to a miserable death. Look

Nursery Manners

Observe proper etiquette when you visit any nursery: don't move tags around; try to avoid dopey questions ("Can you tell me how to design my garden?"); always put plants back exactly where you find them. Don't snap off pieces of plants. Sounds tough? Nursery staff can tell you hair-raising stories about destructive customers. Be one of the respectful people, a true gardener, and they will be helpful beyond your imagination.

for plants rated as hardy for your zone (or colder); otherwise, consider them as annuals.

Within your garden (or your neighbourhood) there can be warmer or cooler areas than the general climate zone. These are called microclimates and every garden usually has several: a dip in the ground is cooler than a sunny spot on the south side of a large rock. You will locate these areas with experience and then you can take advantage of them to "push the zone" as they say, and grow plants that are not normally hardy for you. Similarly, if you live in an area with good snow cover, you can grow many of these plants because they will survive colder temperatures under a deep blanket of snow than they would without it.

Shopping

Winter is the time to plan gardens, look at magazines, catalogues and books, and make plant lists—impossible, wonderful lists. Then hit the real world as early in spring as possible—when the weather is consistently warm and you see buds swelling on the trees or bulbs blooming. This will vary from region to region and year to year. Tempting as it is to go nursery-hopping and to wantonly scoop up anything that catches your eye, resist. By the time you've finished reading this section, you should have a good idea of the plants that will work best in your garden. Make a list, much like a grocery list, and stick to it. You'll want to take some time to gain experience before becoming quixotic about purchases. Once you've got them home, keep your treasures well-watered and in a sheltered spot until it is consistently 10°C at night and the soil has warmed up. Again, this timing will vary across the country. If it gets too cold at night, throw an old sheet over the plants for protection.

Some nurseries and garden centres offer a wide range of plants from trees to bulbs; others specialize in perennials, water plants or even conifers. Some supermarkets and big box stores have extensive plant selections, so shop around. But your plants are only as good as the nursery you choose to patronize. The best will have knowledgeable staff full of helpful suggestions. If you find a place where the regular response to a plant query is a blank look, go somewhere else.

Choose nurseries with pleasing displays of sturdy, healthy-looking plants—no brown leaves, blemished stems, broken branches or damaged bark. The plants should be well-tended, with moist soil, no roots coming out of the bottom of the pots, and no weeds, bugs or signs of disease. Most of all, the plants should be clearly labelled.

Read the Plant Tags

This is like cracking a code: plant tags give you vital information on the plant's growth habits (its ultimate size, rate of growth, bloom time and colour), its origins, hardiness and its light and soil requirements. Reading the tags will also help you to learn the proper botanical names. It may seem easier to latch on to common names, but they change from region to region and can apply to several completely different plants. The Latin moniker describes each individual plant so there's no confusion.

The plant tags usually list the common name followed by the full botanical name, so you will know you are getting exactly the plant you are looking for; the 3-foot (90-centimetre) perennial *Eupatorium rugosum* instead of the 6-foot (1.8-metre) *Eupatorium maculatum*, for example. Remember, all perennials are pretty much the same size when they are cute little babies in the nursery. Similarly, there may be several different species of maple tree on sale, all standing 7 feet (2.1 metres) tall in their nursery containers. But some of them may reach 75 feet (22.8 metres) at maturity; others only 25 feet (7.6 metres). So get to know the proper names of the plants and make a habit of reading the tags. Don't let anyone call you a snob for knowing the following:

GENUS The first word on the tag, it is the name of the plant—for example, *Rosa, Paeonia, Acer*—and is always italicized.

SPECIES The second word, also italicized, usually describes the genus in some way: *Rosa rubrifolia* (a rose with reddish leaves); *Paeonia lutea* (a yellow peony); *Acer japonicum* (a maple from Japan).

CULTIVAR Derived from "cultivated variety," this term refers to a plant produced by crossing two species to produce a hybrid, or by selecting a particular plant for its unusual characteristics and propagating it. The cultivar name is in single quotation marks after the genus and species. Quite often the name is that of the hybridizer or even his mum or some famous person, for example, *Paeonia lactiflora* 'Sarah Bernhardt'.

All good nurseries display plants by their Latin names, so if you are looking for coral bells in perennials, you would look under *H* for *Heuchera*. If you are looking for maples, you would check the first aisle for *Acer* not prowl the *M* section. Tags mean what they say: if the plant needs full sun, then count on it languishing when you put it in the shade. And if the tag gives the plant's ultimate height and spread as 5 feet (1.5 metres), believe it. Watch out for descriptive words or phrases such as "aggressive" and "spread: indefinite." These might be invasive plants

"Buying plants is an art; each one you buy should have both form and function."

SASKATCHEWAN

that grow like weeds, so avoid them unless you put them in containers. Beware especially of variegated goutweed (*Aegopodium podagraria* 'Variegatum'). It can take over your garden in just a couple of seasons.

Choosing Plants

Choosing plants is an art; each one you buy should have both form (a beautiful shape) and function (it fits into your colour scheme or acts as a focal point). When selecting such a range of plants, it helps to have settled on your colour palette. If you are still having trouble defining your palette, try the following: Take something as simple as your favourite indoor cushion or fabric, and select one or two colours from it for outdoor items such as pillows; then incorporate those hues into your plant palette. Or use a favourite colour combination; I'm crazy about lime green and burgundy and will look for *any* plants in those colours. At the nursery use your plant list as a guide and consider adding plants that are aesthetically pleasing and work well together. If they look good together in the shopping cart, they'll look good at home.

Try to pick plants that have bloom, berries, textured bark or some sort of interest for each season, including winter. Most of all, choose plants to suit the site—sunny, shady, wet, sandy and so forth. The surest way to success is getting the right plant in the right place. Given global warming and strange weather patterns, it also makes sense to look for drought-tolerant plants that are less dependent on constant watering.

My general rule for selecting plants is to choose the structural plants first (trees, shrubs and other strong woody plants to give the garden definition); then the vines, tall perennials (useful anchor plants), medium-sized perennials and finally ground covers, annuals and bulbs. I tend to emphasize perennials here because they are the best bargains around: they return year after year, and they get larger and more interesting as they mature.

There is an unwritten gardening rule that says you should always install three or five plants of the same kind. I'd be wary of this—see what does well for you first. You can always buy more.

For Colour

Consider colour first because it affects every plant choice needed to create the layers, textures and patterns that you want for your garden. Colour comes in many forms: through blooms, foliage and the changing seasons. Blooms are obvious; foliage is more subtle with thousands of variations on green, cream, blue, yellow and purple as well as variegations. Foliage is a gardener's best friend, providing constant colour and texture, so focus on it. Choose a basic foliage colour (perhaps gold or burgundy) to use as punctuation throughout the garden, especially in major structural plants.

Choose colours for the times of day when you'll be sitting outside. White is especially luminous late in the day, while hot colours such as red and orange look best in the midday sun. Take a cue from the seasons. The green of emerging foliage in spring is almost a pale yellow, so go for quiet colours; as the greens darken and the sun heats up for summer, use stronger colours.

Pick perennial blooms according to your chosen palette and create planting patterns with harmonious blocks of colour. Don't plunk different colours here and there haphazardly. Make a note when the plants bloom and for how long (about three weeks for most perennials). If you can, buy plants with one flower in bloom so you can be sure of the colour you are getting. Aim to plant several perennials with the same coloured flowers—but with different bloom times—to extend the colour. Put them near an attractive foliage plant so you will still have something to look at when the whole lot go out of bloom. It takes a while to get the hang of it, but experience will tell you which plants to remove from your patterns and which to leave.

To simplify a colour palette, make a monochromatic border, that is, plants of all the same hue. Vary the heights of plants, the blossom size and the blooming period with a mix of woody and herbaceous plants. You will find that plants of the same colour often have quite different tones (for example, there are purply reds and orangey reds) so mix and match with care.

Border Beauty

Treat your borders in a painterly way, with a mix of plants, one colour flowing into the next. Put different plants of the same hue in blocks and use silver, gold or burgundy plants in between to knit them together. For a serene picture, use a variety of blues, purples and white interspersed with silver and burgundy foliage plants to finish the scene. Of course, colours are always changing with the light, the season and particularly adjacent plants, so it takes time to make a success of this kind of border. Handle it one pocket at a time, and remember that plants can be moved very easily.

Top left: A hot border should be placed in full sun and filled with brilliant colours ranging from reds and yellows to purples and oranges. The combination here is of annuals, marigold 'Little Gem' along with potato vine.
Bottom left: A cool border filled with pale tones: blue grasses, silver artemisia and pearly everlasting (*Anaphalis* spp.). Each style fulfills a definite function: one to dazzle (hot) and the other to calm (cool).

BLUE/PURPLE Blues, purples, and greens are considered cool colours and have a calming effect. They also appear to recede, so you can make a small garden appear larger by using lots of blue and purple tones at the far end—the boundary will seem farther away. There are very few true blue flowers; many so-called blue blooms actually lean toward purple.

From purply indigo to pale azure, the blues make beautiful music on their own or accompanying other hues. I'm mad for this colour and consider the following plants must-haves for any garden.

Good structural shrubby plants are Russian sage (*Perovskia atriplicifolia*), growing about 4 feet (1.2 metres) tall, with silver foliage and bright blue blooms in summer, and caryopteris (*Caryopteris* x *clandonensis* 'Kew Blue'), which is a little shorter. Perennial monkshood (*Aconitum*) is utterly poisonous to humans and animals (that's all parts of the plant, especially the roots, seeds and new leaves) but it does attract native bumblebees. It blooms in late summer, and grows up to 5 feet (1.5 metres). The blues of various salvia species are amazing, particularly the long-blooming *S.* x *sylvestris* 'May Night' and *S. verticillata* 'Purple Rain'. It's easy to become an addicted collector of bellflowers (*Campanula*). They come in every size from ground-covering *C. carpatica* 'Blue Clips' to the larger *C. latifolia* that grows to a height of 4 feet (1.2 metres).

GOLD Gold foliage can be used as dramatic punctuation throughout the garden, in sun or shade, or planted with variegated and burgundy foliage. Use it in dark corners where it will give the illusion of dappled sun, or combine it with dark colours to perk them up. Structural plants with the Midas touch include the glorious full-moon Japanese maple (*Acer shirasawanum* 'Aureum'), which grows 20 feet (6 metres) tall, and variegated dogwood (*Cornus alba* 'Aurea') with foliage suffused with yellow on striking red stems, which reaches 7 feet (2.1 metres). For those who live where it's too cold for forsythia and who crave that spring hit of pure yellow, try the ninebark *Physocarpus opulifolius* 'Dart's Gold'. Among perennials, I love the perennial bachelor's buttons *Centaurea montana* 'Gold Bullion' for its bright yellow foliage and brilliant blue cornflower blooms. And there's a veritable gold mine of hostas including *H.* 'Little Sunspot', 'Stained Glass', 'Gold Standard', 'Golden Tusk' and 'Sun Power'.

BURGUNDY Ranging from deep maroon to purple-brown, burgundy is the most versatile of all foliage colours and is my favourite for just that reason. Burgundy plants are stunning paired with silver (*Artemisia* for

BLUE

Monkshood, *Aconitum napellus corneum*

Balloon flower, *Platycodon grandiflorus*

Salvia verticillata, 'Spring Rain'

GOLD

Japanese forest grass, *Hakonechloa macra* 'All Gold'

Sedge, *Carex dolichostachya* 'Gold Fountains'

Barberry, *Berberis thunbergii* 'Aurea'

BURGUNDY

Eastern redbud, *Cercis canadensis* 'Forest Pansy'

Coral bells, *Heuchera* 'Plum Pudding'

Ninebark, *Physocarpus opulifolius* 'Diabolo'

"Burgundy is the most versatile of all foliage colours, and is my favourite for just that reason."

Plants with blue blossoms (top row) are highly prized by most gardeners. Blooms usually hold for a few weeks, but if you look beyond them to the foliage of a plant you will find colour that will last for three seasons and you can plan combinations more easily around that than the temporary joys of blooms.

example), chartreuse (*Euphorbia*) and gold (see page 95). A magnificent small (30-foot/9-metre) tree that would make a strong central focus is Eastern redbud (*Cercis canadensis* 'Forest Pansy') with its large heart-shaped red-purple leaves. A superb background shrub is the ninebark *Physocarpus opulifolius* 'Diabolo', which has intense maroon foliage and pink-tinged white blooms. It grows (rather wildly) to 10 feet (3 metres) but responds to severe pruning. An irresistible perennial is euphorbia (*Euphorbia dulcis* 'Chameleon'). Growing about 2 feet (60 centimetres) tall, it has stunning purple leaves topped by acid-green flowers in spring. It seeds around but is easy to pull out.

ORANGE Vivid hues like orange and red add warmth, lightness and brilliance even in a garden that depends mainly on foliage for colour. Plants that come in hot colours fare best in areas with full sun. In the past, orange roses against red brick and badly executed hot gardens in eye-clawing combinations have discouraged us from this great colour. But, used properly (against bronzes, browns and deep plum), orange plants will add dash to a staid border.

For a fiery autumn-blooming combo, try putting a perennial *Helenium* with annuals such as a purple-leaved dahlia and a climbing nasturtium (*Tropaeolum*). Orange marigolds (*Tagetes*) and purple heliotrope (*Heliotropium*) peak from September to October with powerful intensity. A brilliant annual for summer containers, New Zealand flax (*Phormium*) is available in dozens of shades; *P. tenax* 'Sundowner' is especially striking for its strappy green and orange leaves. Also look for the dramatic *Euphorbia griffithii* 'Fireglow', a perennial that combines blue-green foliage with bright red-orange blooms in summer.

RED True reds are such saturated colours that they turn almost black at a distance and practically disappear in twilight. But red is a stimulating colour and can enliven almost any planting. Contrast rich scarlets with bronze- or copper-foliaged plants such as coral bells (*Heuchera*), bronze fennel or *Physocarpus* 'Coppertina'. It's possible to create a drift of vibrant colour without being garish. Here are three plants with red

ORANGE

Spurge, *Euphorbia griffithii* 'Fireglow'

Sneezeweed, *Helenium* 'Sahins'

New Zealand flax, *Phormium* 'Sundowner Red'

RED

Montbretia, *Crocosmia* 'Lucifer'

Dahlia 'Bishop of Llandaff'

Bee balm, *Monarda* 'Crimson Red'

WHITE

Carolina silver bell, *Halesia carolina*

Star magnolia, *Magnolia stellata*

Lily, *Lilium* 'Casa Blanca'

BLACK

New Zealand flax, *Phormium* 'Platt's Black'

Potato vine, *Ipomea batatas* 'Blackie'

Alternanthera

There is an old garden trick when choosing flowers to plant (both perennials and annuals): find a plant with at least one flower blooming, so that you can more easily match it up with other plants you want to use it with. Use a harmonious colour to start with and keep it as simple as possible: swathes of blues, or oranges or red. Don't sprinkle colour around. It should move smoothly through a garden.

blooms I favour: montbretia (*Crocosmia* 'Lucifer'), *Dahlia* 'Bishop of Llandaff' and bee balm (*Monarda didyma*).

WHITE If you're unsure about colours, an all-white garden is always a good place to start. White gardens complement many settings, from Victorian to contemporary. Install structural shrubs and trees with white blooms for each season, interplanted with white-flowering perennials and annuals and silver-foliaged plants, all of which become more luminous as the day wanes. There are many tones of white, so combine them carefully: a bright white can make a creamier white seem dull and dirty. In multi-toned gardens, you can prevent strong colours from clashing by planting white flowers between them. White is also the first colour the eye goes to, so use white plants as highlights and to draw the attention to specific areas.

Choice trees with white blooms include Pacific dogwood (*Cornus nuttallii*), a native of the West Coast that grows 40 feet (12 metres) high; and Carolina silver bell (*Halesia carolina*), a native with exquisite bells dangling from bare branches in spring and golden foliage in autumn (it grows about 25 feet/7.5 metres tall). For shrubs, I wouldn't be without a star magnolia (*Magnolia stellata*), which has ribbony blossoms in spring, glossy leaves in summer and a pleasing form in winter. The doublefile viburnum *Viburnum plicatum f. tomentosum* 'Shasta' also offers a stunning array of spring flowers and a glorious spreading form.

For perennials, look to candytuft (*Iberis sempervirens*), a tidy, low-growing plant that works well along the edge of a border; Madonna lily (*Lilium candidum*) or *L.* 'Casa Blanca', both of which have a heady scent that carries all over the garden; and Culver's root (*Veronicastrum virginicum*), a native perennial with long spiky blooms attractive to beneficial bugs.

BLACK Ah, the drama of black. It extends from the fashion runway to the garden. Black foliage will pick up undertones of purple, red and brown; try it with lime green and yellow or silver and grey for intense and dramatic combinations. Search out such dark plants as black-leaf elder (*Sambucus* 'Black Beauty'), a handsome sun-loving shrub that grows 6 feet (1.8 metres) tall or more, and *S.* 'Black Lace', a gorgeous smaller form. Perennials such as the daylilies *Hemerocallis* 'Jungle Beauty' and 'Ed Murray' add drama when planted among their yellow and chartreuse cousins. Spiky black mondo grass (*Ophiopogon planiscapus* 'Black Knight')

"Trees and shrubs create the structural framework of the garden."

is small and slow-growing, but planted in a container with brilliant yellow creeping Jenny (*Lysimachia nummularia* 'Aurea'), it's ravishing. Growing 10 inches (25 centimetres) tall, coral bells (*Heuchera* 'Black Beauty' and *H.* 'Obsidian') are spectacular plants that hold their colour well.

For Trees and Shrubs

Trees and shrubs create the structural framework of the garden, so when choosing them, look for form and shape. Does the plant have a strong branching pattern? Will it look good with and without leaves? Can you imagine it with snow on the branches? If it's a conifer, are the branches regular and full, creating an even shape? Make sure the trunk is straight (unless it's a weeping form). When you're at the nursery, choose a tree that doesn't have white plastic wrap girdling the trunk (it's the perfect place for insects to hide). Check all sides of the plant to make sure it looks good from every vantage point.

Trees and shrubs may be sculptural objects in the garden, but they also function as screening plants, hedges and anchors for a large border. In addition to a woody plant's potential purpose, consider the texture and colour of its leaves and bark, whether it has flowers or fruit for seasonal interest, whether it will attract birds, what maintenance it requires and, most important, its ultimate size.

EVERGREENS Evergreens glow with shiny new growth in spring, and in winter they become the focal points of the garden. To ensure a good winter framework, try to make one-third of your total woody plant choices evergreen. They come in a huge range of sizes, shapes and colours. For example, the dwarf white cedar, *Thuja occidentalis* 'Lyonsville', forms a lustrous green ball 3 feet (90 centimetres) across. The lodgepole pine, *Pinus contorta* 'Taylor's Sunburst', develops into a narrow pyramid 15 feet (4.5 metres) tall and has bright yellow candles (upright new growth) in spring. And the Japanese stone pine, *Pinus pumila* 'Dwarf Blue', is a dense, blue horizontal spreader that grows 6 feet (1.8 metres) across. There are even two-toned conifers, such as the Norway spruce, *Picea abies* 'Rubra Spicata', which has red new

growth that changes to red-brown then green. All make fine companions to ornamental grasses, hostas and hydrangeas.

HEDGES AND SCREENS Well-kept hedges bring clean geometry to a garden. Because they need shearing at least twice a season they require some effort to maintain but are beautiful all year round. A classic evergreen hedge can be made from yew (*Taxus*), which has glossy dark needles, tolerates shade and takes pruning very well. Another evergreen, white cedar (*Thuja occidentalis*), is incredibly hardy but needs consistent moisture and full sun to keep its good looks. With its fine texture and tidy habit, boxwood (*Buxus*) is the plant of choice for low-growing formal hedges outlining plantings and paths.

Left unclipped, deciduous shrubs make a more casual-looking hedge and offer a variety of textures and colours without a lot of maintenance. My first vote would go to red osier dogwood (*Cornus sericea*), which has brilliant red stems, tolerates moist conditions and grows up to 6 feet (1.8 metres). Close contenders are blue arctic willow (*Salix purpurea*), which is about the same size, has a fine overall texture and isn't fussy about soil, and, for a low informal hedge, alpine currant (*Ribes alpinum*), which grows to a compact 2 feet (60 centimetres).

Used in a row, tall shrubs can block out the view of an ugly garage next door, hide the barbecue or disguise a shed. In large gardens, they can be planted en masse for dramatic effect. The following shrubs, all growing 10 feet (3 metres) tall, are ideal for all these purposes but are also comely enough to stand alone. Viburnum (*Viburnum* x *pragense*) offers glorious white flowers in spring and handsome foliage. Silver-leaf dogwood (*Cornus alba* 'Elegantissima') has creamy blossoms in early summer, luminous variegated leaves, and red bark in winter. It even grows in deep shade. Beautybush (*Kolkwitzia amabilis*) has arching branches and cascades of pink flowers in late spring.

ROSES Isolating roses from the rest of the garden is a thing of the past, and so are all those eye-searing clashes of colour. Whatever kind of rose you introduce to the garden—from the old-fashioned Gallica to the most

Top left: A charming and very elegant garden shed drowning in vines such as *Clematis x fargesiodes* and climbing roses (always a great combination).
Bottom left: This year-old garden already shows how well an immediate planting of vines can work out. In the foreground is a blue Russian sage, *Perovskia atriplicifolia*; and oakleaf hydrangea, *Hydrangea quercifolia*.

recent David Austen hybrids—they should be integrated into perennial and shrub borders to show off their natural form and growth patterns, whether it's flopping about or climbing. Don't force roses into an unnatural state with perpetual pinning, tying and pruning. Lean them against arbours, pergolas and wooden supports within a border. For best bloom, roses need full sun although rugosa roses will manage on just four hours of sunshine.

Harmonize roses with each other and with stellar companions such as peonies, bleeding hearts, grasses, delphiniums, lupines, Russian sage and shrubs such as butterfly bushes and lilacs. Underplanting roses with hardy geraniums that bloom for most of the summer will cover up the roses' bare stems and keep weeds down. For recurrent bloom, look to Canada's Parkland series of roses ('Winnipeg Parks'). For an old-fashioned classic white, there's 'Blanc Double de Coubert', which is a fragrant repeat bloomer, or go for something with a history such as Rosa mundi rose (*Rosa gallica var. officinalis* 'Versicolor') from 1592, a deep pink splashed with white.

For Vines

Vines improve the look of ugly architecture, provide food for birds, give you green walls in less space than most hedge plants, and can even be used as a ground cover. On your house, they lower the temperature in summer and hold warmth in winter. Paint any structure before planting vines on it and invest in a really good ladder (you'll need it when pruning time comes around).

Vines climb by different means so require different types of support. Twiners such as clematis need lattice or wires to fasten onto; ivy and climbing hydrangea put out aerial roots that cling to the wall so they need a rough surface such as brick or wood. Virginia creeper puts out little adhesive pads that stick to just about any surface but can damage wood siding; a rapid spreader, it can cover a huge blank wall within a few years. Many vines such as wisteria, climbing hydrangea and trumpet vine are vigorous growers requiring strong supports and annual pruning to keep them under control.

My all-time favourite vine is Japanese hydrangea vine (*Schizophragma hydrangeoides*), which resembles climbing hydrangea but is more elegant and less rampant; *S. h.* 'Moonlight' has a gorgeous silver cast to its leaves. And no garden should be without clematis: for spring blooms, try the colourful cultivars of *C. montana*, *C. macropetala* and *C. alpina*.

For summer, look for *C. viticella* 'Betty Corning' (lilac), C. 'Jackmanii' (purple) and the large-flowered hybrids such as 'Niobe' (dark red), 'Comtesse de Bouchaud' (pink) and 'Henryi' (white). For fall, the creamy sweet autumn clematis (*C. terniflora*) is a must.

For Ornamental Grasses
Among the garden world's most versatile plants, ornamental grasses are perfect for the first-time gardener. There's a grass for every season, every soil and every role in the garden, from edger to hedge to focal point. Most grasses are perennial in this country but are worth growing even as annuals. They come in a range of breathtaking colours, including brilliant blues, blood red, copper, bronze and black, and stripes in every shade. Some will seed about but most are well-behaved and take up very little space. They require little care and are not brutish about water. Just give them sun or part-sun, a well-drained site and whack them back to the ground in early spring. They look pathetic for a while and then start growing quickly, making up for their slow start with a superb autumn and winter show.

Plant the huge ones where you can admire their amazing plumes all winter. Smaller grasses mingle companionably with many perennials, especially prairie plants such as coneflowers and black-eyed Susans. Cascading grasses such as Japanese forest grass (*Hakonechloa*) and

Selecting good ornamental grasses can create a wonderful horizon line, as with this mass planting of Eulalia grass, *Miscanthus sinensis*. It is a superb grass, though too large for most gardens. Instead, choose a smaller cultivar that won't spread. There are grasses in every size and colour including blue, red (in the blooms), yellow and variegated.

their relatives, the sedges (*Carex*), look marvellous around a pond. Many grasses are splendid in containers though are not always happy wintering over in them.

Spectacular large grasses include feather reed grass (*Calamagrostis* x *acutiflora* 'Avalanche') at 5 feet (1.5 metres) with elegant white-striped leaves, and Eulalia grass (*Miscanthus sinensis* 'Silberfeder') at 8 feet (2.4 metres) with pale, pinky brown plumes. Serious colour can be found in some of the smaller grasses. Among my favourites are blue oat grass (*Helictotrichon sempervirens*), golden millet grass (*Milium effusum* 'Aureum') and Japanese blood grass (*Imperata cylindrica* 'Red Baron'), all growing less than 2 feet (60 centimetres).

Bamboo is a fast-growing grass that makes an ideal screening plant, focal point, or container specimen (in a really big pot) and is a must for the Japanese garden. There are clumpers that grow from the main root system; and spreaders that should only be used if you have lots of space. To keep them in bounds, plant them in a rubber garbage can sunk into the ground. Black bamboo (*Phyllostachys nigra*) has dramatic black stems and, reaching heights of 20 to 30 feet (6 to 9 metres), will eventually form a small forest. Fountain bamboo (*Fargesia nitida*) is a slow-growing clumper reaching 9 to 10 feet (2.7 to 3 metres) or more. Dwarf white-stripe bamboo (*Pleioblastus fortunei* 'Little Zebra') has eye-catching green and white leaves and grows 2 to 3 feet (60 to 90 centimetres) tall.

For Ground Covers

Ground covers are low-growing plants used to cover a fairly large area. They are usually easy to maintain so are ideal for sites such as steep slopes that are hard to access. Tough and vigorous ground covers such as Siberian barren strawberry (*Waldsteinia ternata*) and sweet woodruff (*Galium odoratum*) are useful to carpet the ground in a shrub border and under trees. Ground covers that will take some foot traffic can be planted along a pathway to add colour and texture; they are also good substitutes for lawn (though they may not stand up to traffic from kids and dogs).

Thymes, especially, offer fabulous colour, scent and wonderful tiny flowers that insects adore. Woolly thyme (*Thymus pseudolanuginosus*) has fragrant, dense, silver foliage and spreads quickly in hot sunny places. Another sun-lover is Scotch moss (*Sagina subulata*), which isn't really a moss but looks as soft; it has starry white flowers. Chamomile

ANNUALS

Clary sage, *Salvia horminum*

Plectranthus 'Mona Lavender'

Canna 'Durban'

HERBS

Lavender, *Lavendula angustifolia* 'Melissa Lilac'

Rosemary, *Rosemarinus officinalis*

Variegated lemon thyme, *Thymus citriodorus variegata*

BULBS

Daffodil, *Narcissus*

Scilla siberica

Species tulip, *Tulipa tarda*

"Annuals have another great quality: many of them seed themselves about in a graceful way without any help from you."

Annuals are every garden's secret ingredient for colour. They bloom all summer long, produce seed and then die. But what a life. Be sure to plant a variety of herbs to mix in with both annuals and perennials. They will add texture and great scent. Each autumn, bulbs should also be planted in spots where there are other plants to disguise the yellowing of the foliage.

(*Chamaemelum nobile*) forms an evergreen mat with ferny leaves and flowers in early summer (deer hate it).

For Annuals

Annuals are a fine addition to every garden. Overused in the past in unattractive public plantings, they are coming back in style. There are so many available now that there is something for every style of garden and every condition possible. Think of wonderful impatiens bringing colour to shady spots where nothing else will grow. Use annuals to fill in spaces until perennials and shrubs mature, or to cover the dying foliage of spring bulbs. Annuals are wonderful container plants on their own or mixed in with perennials. Using annuals in different combinations allows you to experiment with colour schemes inexpensively. The plants don't cost a lot and you can work out in miniature ideas that you might implement on a larger scale next year. Just don't use annuals to the exclusion of all other plants.

Here are some of my favourites. One of the most versatile annuals is coleus (whose proper name is *Solenostemon scutellarioides*). Its many cultivars have striking leaves in every colour from truly black to orange; they tolerate shade and are fabulous in pots. Add drama with *Canna*, tender bulbs that produce huge exotic leaves and hotly coloured flowers for both pots and borders, and honey bush (*Melianthus major*), a dynamic shrub with huge, toothed, silver-green leaves that grows 10 feet (3 metres) tall. Annuals have another great quality: many of them seed themselves about in a graceful way without any help from you. Some of the most reliable are forget-me-nots (*Myosotis*) in blue and pink, clary sage (*Salvia horminum*) in pink, white or purple, and flowering tobacco (*Nicotiana alata*) found in a range of colours.

For Herbs

I like having even just a few herbs in the garden. They are handy for cooking, look terrific and their scent is a big bonus. Herbal foliage colours range from silver to green to deep purple (the basils are notable for this) while blooms are mostly blue, purple and pink. Many herbs,

Far right: Bulbs hold within their unlovely exterior the secret of life. Make sure you pick large, firm bulbs when buying them. Plant them for all three seasons: little ones for an early spring carpet; larger for spring colour and lots of bouquets; then add summer bulbs to containers as well as the border.

especially those from the Mediterranean region, including lavender, rosemary and thyme, have small leaves and can deal with summer drought. All need plenty of sun.

Herbs look lovely woven throughout the garden because they offer wonderful textures (particularly the sages) and attract beneficial bugs. But a mix of herbs can also make an ornamental raised bed or a stunning container. In fact, enthusiastic spreaders such as mint should never be grown in anything else but a pot.

For Bulbs

There are little bulbs and big bulbs, spring-blooming bulbs and summer-blooming bulbs. All enhance a garden's tapestry effect: think of them as the fine embroidery. Small spring-blooming bulbs such as glory-of-the-snow (*Chionodoxa*), winter aconite (*Eranthis*) and snowdrops (*Galanthus*) bloom first and can be tucked here and there under shrubs and trees for an early splash of colour. The bigger spring bulbs such as daffodils and tulips bloom a little later, and of course the summer-blooming ones add to that season's display. Since bulbs are available in a range of colours, heights and bloom times, some coordination is needed. Once again, work out a colour scheme. Blue and yellow is an easy basic combination, then add burgundy or pink or lime. Or try purple and green with white; or pink and purple; or orange and blue.

Buy dozens—hundreds if you have the time to plant them—of little bulbs such as intense blue *Scilla* and grape hyacinths (*Muscari*). (If you have too many to plant at once, store them in the fridge or in a cool shed, anywhere they won't get too warm or freeze.) Plant them like a stream flowing through other bulbs and perennials. They will naturalize (multiply and spread) all by themselves. Use them along the edge of a border backed up by species (small, early-blooming) tulips. Pop them in obscure corners, even in a shady woodland—they will bloom before the trees leaf out—or layer them in containers. The big bulbs such as tulips and daffodils should be clustered almost like bouquets in harmonious arrangements, with one colour melting into the next. And the more bulbs the better (hundreds if you have room). As they are large, plant them at least a foot (30 centimetres) away from shrubs.

For Containers

Traditionally, only annuals were used in containers. In the modern garden, pots are a very contemporary way of handling perennials, shrubs

and even trees. This is driven by a need to maximize our compact urban spaces with rooftop and balcony gardens. But gardens of every size should have containers; they fit in anywhere and can be moved around for a great many kinds of drama.

Perfect trees for pots are Japanese maples, unmatched for their form, shape and colour. They need a container at least two to three times the width of the pot the plant came in from the nursery, and in most areas, will have to spend the winter in a garage or shed. They may not reach their full size in a pot but will still add astounding beauty to any style garden.

PERENNIALS I wouldn't have pots without hostas. They are so tough and adaptable and work on their own or in combination with other plants. Sumptuous specimens include 'Krossa Regal', 'Regal Splendor' and the blue 'Halcyon'. Smaller cultivars that I adore are 'Queen Josephine', 'Elvis Lives' and 'Spilt Milk'. A new generation of tiny ones such as 'Tattoo' and 'Bitsy Green' can be used like a bouquet in a bowl-shaped container. Coral bells (*Heuchera*) are ideal filler plants, with leaves ranging from mottled green through copper and burgundy to almost black. For sunny, windy locations, go for hens and chicks (*Sempervivum*), rosette-forming succulents ranging in colour from deep red to silver grey. And for shady spots, you can't beat ferns such as lady fern (*Athyrium filix-femina* var. *angustum* 'Lady in Red') and the silver-splashed Japanese painted fern (*A. niponicum* var. *pictum*).

ANNUALS There are fresh and exciting ways to design a container of annuals; just follow these few simple rules. Never place your focal point plant (often a dramatic spiky plant such as the over-used *Dracaena*) in the middle of the pot. Put it to one side to add character. Tuck at least three or five summer bulbs into each container. In six weeks, they will be poking up among the maturing annuals or perennials. This seems obvious, but never mix plant types; keep like with like. Woodland plants do not go with tropicals (read the information on the tags or ask someone when you buy them). For contrast of colours, plant a vine to grow through the other plants. Top off with a pea gravel mulch to discourage the weevils and slugs that can destroy container plants.

In addition to coleus (see page 107), I would always want *Plectranthus* species, especially P. 'Mona Lavender' with its green and purple leaves and neon blue-purple flowers, and sweet potato vine (*Ipomoea batatas*

This container glows with the warmth of orange, deep burgundy and magenta flowing one into the other. At the rear off to one side: *Canna* ' African Sundown'; moving forward: *Phormium* 'Glowing Embers'; in bloom *Coleus* 'Rustic Orange'; *Acalypha* (copperleaf) and spilling over the side is the black potato vine Ipomea 'Blackie'. There are also summer bulbs; *Geranium* 'Vancouver Gold' and a grass called *Stipa tenuissima* which can't be seen.

Top right: An effective shade plant is the Japanese painted fern (*Athyrium niponicum* var. *pictum*).
Top far right: One of the new generations of Brunnera. The one shown here is 'Jack Frost' and an even better one is 'Looking Glass'; both hold their lovely silver overlay all summer long.
Bottom right: The native *Geum triflorum* in bloom, surrounded by several hardy geraniums.

'Blackie'), which is, bar none, the best annual vine; it looks lovely spilling over the edge of a container. *I. b.* 'Marguerite' is the golden form.

For Shade

Don't think the plant palette is limited to sun-lovers, thousands of plants prefer shade. Here, blooms are less important than foliage—and why not, when leaf colours range from silver and gold to burgundy, purple and blue-green. Variegated leaves with pale spots, splashes and stripes will light up a shady corner, but don't put too many variegated plants together—it looks revolting. Look for contrasting leaf shapes and textures, too: the large heart-shaped silvery leaves of *Brunnera* 'Jack Frost' set against feathery ferns, for example.

With their range of sizes, shapes and colours, hostas are must-haves, of course. Hellebores are also splendid shade plants with peony-like foliage and blooms for almost every season: *Helleborus niger* in winter, *H.* x *sternii* in early spring, and *H. viridis* in spring through early summer. Fabulous ferns include Christmas fern (*Polystichum acrostichoides*), so named because it remains green in December, and licorice fern (*Polypodium glycyrrhiza*), so called because its rhizomes (underground stems) have a sweetish flavour.

A shady combination I love is a burgundy-leafed black snakeroot such as *Cimicifuga* 'Black Negligee' and one of the lungworts, perhaps *Pulmonaria* 'Excalibur' with its elegant silver leaves. For semi-shade, you can't beat the hardy geranium, *Geranium pratense* 'Hocus Pocus', which has smoky leaves and lavender flowers, set against the smashing lime green leaves of the coral bells, *Heuchera* 'Lime Rickey'.

RHODODENDRONS These are called broad-leafed evergreens and, to thrive, must have loose acidic soil, consistent moisture and dappled shade. If you have less than ideal conditions but still want their showy spring blooms, try the tougher little-leaf (or lepidote) forms which will take some sun. *Rhododendron* 'PJM' is an ironclad starter plant with rosy purple blooms. R. 'Ramapo' is a small delicate-looking but very tough plant with purple blooms. For large leaf (or elepidote) forms, try *R.* 'Catawbiense Album' and *R. yakushimanum*; or on the West Coast, *R. auriculatum*, which puts out scented white flowers as late as August.

For Native Plants

More and more gardeners are looking for plants native to their particular region. It especially makes sense for gardens in the country and at the cottage, where "citified" plants would look out of place. Native plants have a natural beauty, attract insects like crazy, and require little coddling in the garden. If you happen to find flowers such as native orchids and trilliums growing on your property, don't try to move them, just enjoy them and throw a little mulch on the area in fall. Explore your local landscape to learn what plants grow in harmony and the conditions they prefer. Note that many familiar plants such as Queen Anne's lace are not native but introduced exotics taking over aggressively wherever they can.

Never buy native plants from people who rip them out of the wilderness to sell them. Look for a nursery that propagates them and can guarantee this; there are many growers specializing in native plants now and most nurseries devote a section to them.

Two sturdy silver shrubs that will sparkle in any sunny setting are silver sagebrush (*Artemisia cana*) and four-wing saltbush (*Atriplex canescens*). Perennial standouts include Joe Pye weed (*Eupatorium fistulosum*), a gigantic form reaching 8 feet (2.4 metres) or more with huge blooms that butterflies adore, and goldenrod (*Solidago*), a much reviled plant that does not cause allergies and has glorious cultivars such as 'Golden Wings' and 'Cloth of Gold'. Sun-loving coneflowers (*Echinacea*) are drought-tolerant and suit all types of soil; in addition to

the pink shades of the many species, now there are exciting cultivars in orange, yellow, white and purple. For a classic prairie look, put them with black-eyed Susans (*Rudbeckia hirta*), yellow lance-leaf coreopsis (*Coreopsis lanceolata*) and bright orange blanket flowers (*Gaillardia*).

For a Healing or Contemplative Garden

The focus in this type of garden is on sensory appeal, so ideal plants include those with lots of fragrance (such as roses, daphnes, lilies and flowering tobacco); touchable plants (lamb's ears, *Celosia*, peonies, *Artemisia*); and colourful plants (especially in the calming tones of white, blue, pink, peach and purple, rather than hot hues). Herbs such as rosemary, basil and mint provide not only scent and texture but also taste, while ornamental grasses and trees such as trembling aspen and willows offer a gentle, rustling sound.

For Autumn Colour

Spring and summer are easy to choose for because so many plants flower at that time. Having a good-looking, colourful garden in fall and winter is harder to achieve but is so desirable in this country. There are some gorgeous late-blooming perennials, but autumn really belongs to the spectacular foliage colour of trees such as the maples (especially Japanese maple), sweetgum, serviceberry and Katsura tree. Shrubs are not to be outshone: redvein enkianthus (*Enkianthus campanulatus*) has flaming yellow, orange and red autumn colour and, in spring, bell-like

Mixing Foliage

When selecting plants think carefully about different sizes of leaves. They are just as significant as blooms, and have their own personality and texture. Too many small leaves grouped together make a dizzying combination; too many variegated ones make the plants seem sick. Combine some large ones with smaller forms and shapes. Foliage will last three seasons so it's a very important element in a garden design.

"Don't be too hasty in cleaning up the garden in fall."

Berry Bounty

Make sure your garden includes plenty of shrubs and vines with berries that stay on for most of the winter. You will enjoy their colour until the birds get desperate and they become a source of food.

Far right: Winter has its own magic, especially in the shape of small trees and shrubs. When plants are lit up with fairy lights they can be breathtaking. Make sure there's a well-grounded outdoor plug so you can put up some night lights, even if you can't afford a full lighting treatment.

blooms in a pale almost lingerie pink with darker striations. It grows slowly to 10 feet (3 metres). Slightly smaller, oakleaf hydrangea (*Hydrangea quercifolia*) has sumptuous, lace-cap type flowers in late summer, rich fall foliage and shaggy, exfoliating bark (bark that peels and shreds) in winter.

My favourite fall-blooming perennials must include the stately white Japanese anemone (*Anemone* x *hybrida* 'Honorine Jobert'); orchid-like toad lilies (*Tricyrtis*), now in many new forms; and yellow wax bells (*Kirengeshoma koreana*), which has pale yellow blooms in September and pairs wonderfully with magenta foliage plants.

For a total surprise, plant colchicums (*Colchicum autumnale*), often called autumn crocuses, in early fall. Within a couple of weeks, the bulbs will produce stalks topped by pinky-purple blooms. The leaves will follow in spring, and next autumn there will be even more flowers.

For Winter Interest

Besides evergreens, look for bark with colour and/or texture. Shrubby dogwoods come with red, orange, acid yellow or deep green twigs. For specimens with exfoliating bark look no further than the lovely tree, maackia (*Maackia amurensis*), whose emerging leaves in spring are a ghostly grey; seven-son flower (*Heptacodium miconioides*), a big shrub or small tree that blooms in autumn; and paperbark maple (*Acer griseum*) whose glorious cinnamon orange peeling bark only improves with age.

Don't forget berries, they light up the winter landscape until the birds get too hungry. Look for the orange fruit of firethorn and mountain ash; the scarlet berries of cotoneaster and winterberry (a deciduous holly); and the startling purple clusters of beautyberry. Left untouched, the plumes of ornamental grasses will catch the light and snow all winter. Don't be too hasty in cleaning up the garden in fall. Many perennial seedheads (such as those of coneflowers, clematis and anemones) are decorative and provide food for birds.

My Ten Essential Plants

If you have read through all the above and still cannot make up your mind about where to start, use these plants, all of which are quite readily available. In my estimation, no gardener should live without them. This collection includes small trees, shrubs and perennials, along with my favourite grass, and will make an excellent framework on which to build.

1. Serviceberry (*Amelanchier canadensis*) is a four-season small native tree or large shrub. Growing up to 21 feet (6.3 metres) tall in sun or shade, it is bedecked with sparkling white flowers in spring, delicious purple black berries in summer, and scarlet foliage in autumn. The bark is a velvety striated grey in winter. Superb as a stand-alone specimen, it also makes a fine screening plant in a woodland setting. Zone 4.

2. Japanese maple (*Acer palmatum* 'Dissectum Atropurpureum') is a low-growing (8 to 10 feet/2.4 to 3 metres), wide-spreading tree with finely cut purple leaves that turn neon orange in autumn. Like all Japanese maples, it needs shade from the hottest sun. Zone 6.

3. Black elder (*Sambucus* 'Black Lace') is the plant to have if you can't grow Japanese maples. It has the same glorious cutleaf foliage, except that it's an amazing purple-black. It also has pink lightly fragrant flowers in early summer followed by black berries that birds love. This one grows from 8 to 10 feet (2.4 to 3 metres) high. It needs either full sun or part shade to maintain the foliage colour.

4. Viburnum (*Viburnum plicatum* 'Summer Snowflake') is an incredibly versatile shrub that grows anywhere from 4 feet (1.2 metres) to 7 feet (2.1 metres), depending on how rich the soil is and how warm the zone. White lace-cap flowers will bloom from June until the autumn frosts blast them away. Zone 5.

5. White snakeroot (*Eupatorium rugosum* 'Chocolate') is a perennial with deep purple-brown foliage all summer and a froth of white flowers in autumn. Growing about 4 feet (1.2 metres) tall, it likes moist soil in sun or part shade. Zone 4.

6. Bowman's root (*Gillenia trifoliata*) is a native perennial from Eastern

Your Own Essential List

My essential plant list includes the items that I think are absolutely necessary for the best of all gardens. If you aren't in the right zone, find a plant that comes close to those on the list. Soon you'll be making your own essential plant list. Just remember to always make sure you select plants that have a good form and look splendid in as many seasons as possible. Winter bark and berries, spring and summer blooms, autumn leaves and foliage. A combination of all these items is what you're after.

Canada with brilliant flowers in June and gorgeous autumn tones. It reaches about 3 feet (90 centimetres) in sun or shade. Zone 5.

7. Black snakeroot (*Cimicifuga* 'James Compton') is a spectacular member of a family of perennial black bugbanes. Growing to about 32 inches (80 centimetres), it has deep purple-brown leaves with fragrant white bottlebrush blooms on long stems. It likes sun and rich soil but will tolerate shade and still retain its colour. Zone 4.

8. Large merrybells (*Uvularia grandiflora*) is an eastern woodland native perennial of extraordinary beauty that grows about 2 feet (60 centimetres) tall. Its lily-like nodding yellow bells bloom in May amid long, gracefully dangling leaves. Zone 3.

9. Golden Japanese forest grass (*Hakonechloa macra* 'Aureola') is a perfect perennial, growing in sun or shade, in a border or in a container. It forms a cascading mound 10 inches (25 centimetres) high. Normally hardy to Zone 6, it could grow in Zone 5 in a sheltered spot with a protection of winter mulch. And it's well worth using as an annual in colder areas.

10. Hosta (*Hosta* 'June') with its blue-edged leaves is a standout among many great hostas. The centre of the leaves starts out cream and gradually turns a stunning chartreuse. The leaves are topped by violet flowers in midsummer. It reaches a height of 15 inches (38 centimetres) and a spread of 3 feet (90 centimetres). Zone 3.

If you have room, add one magnificent large native tree to that list. I live at the edge of the Carolinian forest so my choice is a Kentucky coffee tree (*Gymnocladus dioica*), which grows to 70 feet (21 metres) and has grand feathery leaves about 3 feet (90 centimetres) long resembling a prehistoric fern.

Having made up your mind what colour palette will suit your garden, what foliage hues to thread through it, and the trees, shrubs, perennials, annuals, bulbs and grasses you need for a glorious multi-layered garden, you can head off to the nurseries confident that the plants you select will work in your overall scheme. The next step is getting them in the ground.

READ PLANT TAG
CAREFULLY

SOAK PLANTS WELL

TRIM MUSHY ROOTS

PLANT WHEN IT'S
COOL

WATER WELL
AT PLANTING
TIME

MULCH
QUICKLY

How to Plant

Woody Plants
Perennials
Annuals
Bulbs
Containers
Under a Tree

How to Plant

Putting a plant into the ground properly will take it a long way down the road to survival and health. The sight of a well-planted garden means someone cares. Dig a hole that's the same depth as the plant and twice as wide. Water the hole to check for drainage. Then pop in the plant and water well again. Voilà, a happy plant.

PLANTING IS NOT JUST A MATTER OF STICKING PLANTS IN THE GROUND. Learn to plant well and your plants will thrive. Plant badly and you court disappointment. The best method is to install the entire garden in layers. Start with trees, move down to shrubs, then plant the tall perennials and medium-sized perennials, and finally ground covers and annuals. (If it's fall, you can tuck spring-blooming bulbs among them all as you proceed.)

When to Plant

In most parts of the country nurseries sell a good selection of plants beginning in early May through September, and it is safe to plant during these months. Still, the optimum planting times are spring and fall when temperatures are cool and the ground moist.

Most woody plants, especially evergreens, can be planted in fall but some trees such as magnolia, oaks, hornbeams and beech should be planted in spring only. Perennials can be planted any time from May to September except for ornamental grasses, which will get better established when planted in spring and summer. Generally, annuals are heat lovers and should be planted outside only after all danger of frost is past. Bulbs that bloom in spring are planted the previous fall. Summer-blooming bulbs are planted in spring. If in doubt, check with your local nursery staff on what to plant when, especially in your region.

Equipment

You don't need a lot of tools, even for a high-maintenance garden. First, wear a good pair of gloves. I love the flexible kind that move with the hand because I'm more likely to keep them on. It's also a good idea to get a rubber pair for working with roses and pond plants, and leather ones for working with evergreens. Next, the principal tools you will need for planting are a strong transplanting spade with a deep dish and a sharp edge, and a transplanting trowel with an extra long dish for working in tight spaces between plants.

In addition to the above, you should have a pair of good secateurs or hand clippers, a pair of cheap secateurs (as a backup when you can't

Root Balls

Trees come from the nursery in two ways: container grown, where their root systems have always lived in a confined space or balled-and-burlapped, which means they've been grown in a field. Balled trees have been dug up and their roots protected by burlap. No matter what anyone tells you, remove the burlap before planting. Generally speaking balled-and-burlapped trees should be planted only in spring and autumn.

find the expensive ones), a pair of long-handled bypass loppers to cut any branch or stem more than half an inch (1.25 centimetres) thick, a pair of garden shears, and a child-sized wooden rake to drag debris out of inconvenient spots. It's easy to indulge yourself by buying different kinds of pruners, shovels and trowels, but you can garden very well with only these.

Getting Started

First, set all the plants in their pots out on the ground where you think they should go and move them around to fine-tune their relationships with regard to their colour, texture, bloom time and, most important, their ultimate size. You want pleasing height variations, harmonious colour combinations, contrasting foliage textures (large and small; fuzzy and smooth) and overall balance. This is a slow and thoughtful process so don't rush it. It often helps to do "mini-groupings" of three plants (trees, shrubs and certainly perennials and annuals) in a triangular arrangement so you avoid stiff rows, and build from there with additional triangles. Once you have the plants placed, turn each one so it presents its most attractive side (called the face) to the viewer. Repeat this positioning process with the shrubs, perennials and annuals.

Woody Plants

How to Plant a Tree

Soak the tree's root ball as soon as you get it home by dunking it in its pot or burlap wrapping in a big tub of water or, if it's too big to do that, letting a hose gently dribble into the root ball for an hour. Measure and dig a hole that's the same depth as the root ball and at least two to three times as wide. Loosen the soil at the bottom but don't add any amendments (unless you have clay soil, in which case you can add a layer of coarse grit and fine horticultural sand to the bottom of the hole to help with drainage). Scientists have found that if the soil used to back fill around the root ball is much richer than the soil beyond the planting hole, the roots will be reluctant to spread, and could go into shock when they finally venture out and hit the poorer soil. That is why enriching the entire planting area first is so important (see page 34).

Take the tree out of its container or, if the root ball is wrapped in burlap (in the trade this is referred to as balled-and-burlapped), remove the burlap altogether. Some nurseries recommend leaving it on. Don't— any fabric left exposed will wick moisture away from the roots.

A well-organized tool shed is not only attractive, as this one is, but it will mean you won't have to search around for tools. Never put tools away without cleaning them first. Some essential tools are transplanting and border spades, a rake, a watering can, secateurs and a cultivator.

Plant so the base of the trunk is a couple of inches (5 centimetres) higher than ground level. This is called planting proud and it prevents water from collecting around the trunk and causing rot. If you plant the base below soil level, the tree will start to struggle in a week or two. A friend of mine has a rhyming reminder: "Plant a tree high and it won't die; plant it low and it won't grow."

Carefully tamp the soil around the root ball to get rid of any air pockets. Turn on the hose and let the water dribble slowly and gently around the plant for an hour or more. Repeat this watering a couple of times a week, using a trowel to check how moist it is down beside the root ball (the principal cause of trees dying young is insufficient water in their first year). Do this until you see new growth, then water thoroughly once a week. Spread your favourite mulch over a generous area around the tree, keeping mulch a few inches away from the trunk. Healthy trees planted properly don't need staking (fastened to a stake to hold it upright). A bit of movement in the wind helps to strengthen the root system. Don't cut back any of the tree's branches; you may remove buds and delay bud break.

"Make sure you have the shrub's most attractive face showing."

How to Plant a Hedge

Measure the distance you want the hedge to cover so you can calculate how many plants you need. For example, a low boxwood hedge starts with small plants set about 6 inches (15 centimetres) apart. Taller evergreens such as yews, junipers and cedars are planted 18 to 24 inches (45 to 60 centimetres) apart for a formal hedge. Deciduous hedges such as privet or dwarf arctic willow can be planted farther apart. Once you know the specific hedge plant you want, you can also ask for help at the nursery in estimating the number of plants required. Follow the instructions for tree planting and water regularly. A deciduous hedge can be cut back to 8 inches (20 centimetres) in height at planting to promote strong bushy growth. Evergreens should be trimmed only in late spring.

How to Plant a Shrub

Make sure you have the shrub's most attractive face showing (the side of the plant with the fullest growth and most pleasing shape) and then follow the instructions for tree planting.

Plants with Special Instructions

ROSES If you get roses by mail order, they will arrive in early spring with bare roots (no soil on them). They might look unredeemable but don't be put off. Keep them moist in a cool dark location and plant them as soon as possible. Just before planting, add a small amount of fish fertilizer to a bucket of cold water and soak the roots overnight. Dig a generous hole leaving a small mound in the centre of the bottom. Trim off any mushy or broken roots. Tease apart the roots and set the plant on the mound spreading the roots outward. Check the stem for a line indicating the soil level at which the plant was grown (the stem will be lighter in colour above it and darker below). If you live in Zone 7 or warmer, plant it level with that line. If you are in a colder zone, plant it 2 or 3 inches (5 to 8 centimetres) deeper. Adjust the size of the mound to get the correct level. Roses purchased in containers have root balls and can be planted like shrubs; just observe the same planting-level rules as with bare-root roses.

Far right: When planting a shrub make sure the hole is the same depth as the root of the shrub and at least twice as wide. Make sure the top of the plant will be slightly higher than the level of the soil so that water runs away from the plant rather than pooling around the stem. Tamp down gently and dribble in water for an hour to make sure it's wet below the root system. Never add anything to the bottom of the hole, instead top-dress with compost.

Add a couple of banana peels to the planting hole (they give a boost of potassium). Tamp the soil around and over the roots, water thoroughly and mulch. Cut back the stems (called canes) by about a third, to where you see a bud on the outside of the cane (called an outward-growing bud). Make a clean cut at a 45-degree angle just above and away from the bud.

RHODODENDRONS Rhododendrons are forest plants: they need acidic soil, protection from wind and the company of trees such as pines and oaks. They will not fare well under maples or willows (too much root competition) or black walnuts (whose roots exude a toxin called juglone). Never put them close to the house foundation: the soil is likely to be far too alkaline.

Rhodos need loose, friable soil high in organic matter that will provide excellent drainage and aeration. If you don't have these conditions naturally, use raised beds: dig down 8 inches (20 centimetres) and put down a layer of gravel; then add enough sandy soil, coarse bark chips and organic matter such as compost in equal portions to raise the bed 12 inches (30 centimetres) above ground level.

Soak the roots well before planting (as you would a tree). Make a hole no deeper than the root ball and about twice as wide, and gently plunk in the rhodo, making sure it is planted proud. Loosely fill in the soil around the root ball; don't tamp it too firmly. (Never hoe or cultivate close to rhodos as their delicate rootlets are close to the surface.) To encourage a shapely plant, pinch back new shoots (cut off the tips) but stop doing so after July 1 so that next year's buds can form.

CLEMATIS Plant clematis as you would a shrub—just be sure you set the root ball at least 2 or 3 inches (5 or 8 centimetres) below soil level and mulch with plenty of organic matter. When a clematis is first planted, the whole plant should be chopped back to about 4 inches (10 centimetres) in height; it's painful to do but the result is a stronger plant. In subsequent years, follow the pruning instructions on page 151.

Rose Food

When planting roses, include some banana peels to add potassium to the soil. A sprinkle of potash (wood ashes contain this element) around the plant will add magnesium. Epsom salts added to the soil will feed roses and tomatoes. 1 tsp (12 ml) in a pint (.5 L) of water makes a good foliar spray. Add nitrogen with manure and compost.

This garden features the perfect place to plant roses—over an arch and in full sun. Roses need a minimum of six hours of sun. Don't fool yourself into thinking you can stick them in the shade—the results will be disappointing. Behind this shower of climbing roses there's a Japanese variegated willow, *Salix* 'Hakuro Nashiki'.

Perennials and Annuals

Proper planting of a perennial begins with a large enough hole—one as deep as the root ball and three times wider. Give the pot a good thwack on the side to release the plant. Break up the soil in the bottom of the hole (but don't add any fertilizer or manure), and water the hole. Let the water drain away. Loosen the plant's roots if they are tightly entwined and set the plant in the hole, making sure the base of the plant is right at soil level. Back fill the hole with soil, tamping it firmly with the heel of your hand to get rid of air pockets. Water thoroughly and mulch.

If planting new perennials in fall (when many nurseries have their sales), cut off any blooms so the plant will shunt its energy into establishing strong roots.

Plants with Special Instructions

PEONIES Peonies are long-lived, easy-care perennials that just need sun, fertile well-draining soil and a regular dollop of compost. The key to having luxurious blooms is shallow planting. Follow the instructions for planting perennials—but make sure peonies are planted an inch (2.5 centimetres) or so higher than soil level. Japanese tree peonies are different; these are more like a woody shrub and do not die back to the ground. They need to be planted very deeply. You can bury them 3 or 4 inches (8 or 12 centimetres) up the stem and they will be fine.

BAMBOO Bamboos are best planted from June through midsummer in a sunny spot with moist but not waterlogged soil. Follow the instructions for planting perennials, confining spreading-type bamboos in a container sunk into the ground. An ordinary lawn grass fertilizer can be applied to give a boost of nitrogen, but a rich organic mulch is preferable. In tough winters, hardy bamboos might die back to the ground but should resprout from the base in spring.

Planting Ground Covers

Measure the area you want to cover to figure out how many plants you need to buy. Check the ultimate spread of the plant you are considering and work from there. A good nursery person can give a quick calculation depending on what plants you are using. The denser the planting, the more quickly it will fill in. Follow the instructions for planting perennials. You can divide most ground covers, including Scotch moss and the mat-forming types like sweet woodruff, straight out of their containers.

Top left: A screen covered with a great clematis going full tilt. When planting clematis, make sure the growing start of the plant is about an inch (2.5 cm) below the level of the soil. Cut back the vines to let the root grow strong.
Bottom left to right: How to make a plant support: Put sticks into the ground in four places around the plant, add a circle of woven sticks or wire and gather the tall sticks at the top. This will make an attractive support for the plant to grow inside.

Ground covers such as chamomile (above left) and sweet woodruff (above right), can make a beautiful lawn alternative.

Divide them in half, or more, and plant each little division as a separate plant. To increase ground covers, take cuttings (little pieces with some roots on them) from established plants. Then pop them into a freshly prepared area.

Planting Annuals

Most annuals are heat loving so they should only be planted when the soil has warmed up and there is no danger of frost. In the ground, plant them the same way as perennials. Since you should plant perennials and shrubs far enough apart to allow for their ultimate height and spread, annuals are invaluable for filling in the spaces for a season or two until the more permanent plants fill out. For planting annuals in containers, see page 135.

Annuals that grow from bulbs (such as caladiums and calla lilies), rhizomes (cannas) and tubers (dahlias and tuberous begonias) all need to be planted relatively close to the surface of the soil. Loosen the soil in the planting area to a depth of 12 inches (30 centimetres) and add lots of compost. Dig a hole three times deeper than the diameter of the bulb, rhizome or tuber. Set the tuber horizontally in the hole with the buds (the little bumps on the tuber) facing up. Press it down with your hand to make sure it has good soil contact, cover with soil and water well.

The fall chrysanthemums that fill all the garden centres with their bright yellow, magenta, pink, white and rust-red blooms are practically irresistible. In most of the country, they should be treated as annuals; they are perennial in only the warmest zones. Still, they add a welcome hit of colour so tuck them in next to ornamental grasses or colourful

Planting bulbs (above left), starts with a sensible size hole, usually three times the height of the bulb itself. Make sure the bottom of the hole is loose, and then back fill with soil and top-dress with compost. Bulbs don't need any more than that. The deeper the hole, the later the bulb will bloom so plant with different depths in mind to achieve great results (above right).

autumn shrubs such as fothergilla or oakleaf hydrangea, remove the spent blossoms regularly, and cut them back if they start looking weary. They'll bloom until frost takes them.

Planting Herbs

Most herbs (whether annual or perennial) need sun and excellent drainage. They can be planted in spring and summer throughout the garden in containers or in raised beds: use wood or stones to make an edging for the bed, lay down a layer of gravel for drainage, and fill with a mix of two parts topsoil to one part sand. Raised beds will warm up before the ground does, allowing you to get a head start with your herbs in spring.

Bulbs

Spring-blooming bulbs are bought and planted from mid-fall, into early winter if the ground is still workable (summer bulbs are planted in spring). Bulbs should be planted right after purchase, but if that's not possible, keep them in the fridge or a cool shed until planting time.

The main rules for planting bulbs: they must have good drainage and they should be placed at a depth equal to three times the height of the bulb itself. The bulb is planted pointy side up. If you can only afford fifty bulbs this year, mass them for a good display. When they bloom, take pictures so you will know where they are and where you will need more next year.

Most bulbs need sun but you can plant them under deciduous trees and near shrubs because they will bloom before the trees or shrubs leaf out and shade them. However, some bulbs such as tulips like hot dry

"Keeping squirrels from digging up your bulbs is a challenge—screaming and yelling does not work."

summers, so plant them in sunny spots next to a driveway or patio rather than a shady area that may be too cool and moist for them.

Don't plant bulbs in regimented rows, toss them on the ground and plant them where they drop and roll. Or plant them in flowing bands like rivers through the garden, or in drifts (large irregularly shaped clusters). To create a succession of bloom in one space, layer bulbs. Dig a wide hole a good 8 to 10 inches (20 to 25 centimetres) deep. Break up the soil in the bottom and put a layer of big bulbs such as tulips or daffodils. Cover them with a layer of soil and then add a layer of smaller bulbs such as dwarf iris or grape hyacinths at a depth of about 5 inches (12 centimetres). Back fill with soil.

Water any bulb planting thoroughly and spread a layer of mulch over the area. Keeping squirrels from digging up your bulbs is a challenge— screaming and yelling does not work. I know people who give them peanuts as a bribe. You can try to foil them by adding a deep layer of leaves or scatter thorny branches over the area (don't worry about the bulbs, they can find their way through anything). Or lay a piece of chicken wire or hardware cloth (it's like a metal screen) over the soil, hold it down with bricks and add mulch. It's no longer correct to sprinkle around heavy-duty cayenne pepper because it can damage the squirrels' eyes—and you can be sure someone's watching you. You can try planting bulbs the critters don't like such as daffodils, fritillaries, alliums, grape hyacinths, snowdrops and Scilla; in my experience, the squirrels still pull these out of the ground, inspect them and toss them aside.

Another challenge with bulbs is finding a way to disguise their dying foliage. This must be left on until it is completely yellowed as it is feeding the bulb for next year's bloom. The foliage of larger bulbs hangs on until you want to just rip out the whole lot and be done with it. Resist this temptation and DON'T braid, twist, put rubber bands on or otherwise tidy these leaves or they won't be able to feed the bulb. It's better to plant these bulbs near (but not too near) perennials, which will grow up and hide the dying leaves, and in places where you can plunk in some fantastic new annuals.

The Amazing Allium

Alliums are great bulbs to choose. They will naturalize (that is they multiply and spread themselves around). A dozen allium bulbs in one spot will, in a few years, be a great display. Since they are so slender they can be tucked in around shrubs and trees without disturbing feeder roots. Put them with Euphorbia *spp. (the purple ones go so well with the acid yellow tones of the latter).*

Little Bulbs

Small bulbs such as *Scilla*, crocuses and grape hyacinths can be planted in wide shallow holes by the dozen rather than individually. Because they multiply endlessly (a process called naturalizing), they will create a wonderful carpet of bloom in a few years. Crocuses look especially lovely popping out of a lawn: simply peel back a rectangle of sod about a foot (30 centimetres) square. Loosen the soil and tuck in a handful of bulbs, spread out so they are not touching. Firm the soil over them and replace the turf. Water well. Just remember in spring that you can't mow the lawn until the crocuses' leaves have completely died back.

Big Bulbs

The easiest planting plan is to take a dozen bulbs of each colour and plant them in groups gliding harmoniously from one colour to the next. Put flared, striped and frilled tulips together. They are such show-offs you may want to have a special section for them. Otherwise pick one colour and add a few to your more conventional tulips.

Containers

Containers are invaluable for patios and balconies; in the garden, a single one can be used as a focal point, or a few can be clustered in an artful arrangement. Anything can be used as a plant container, from an antique sap bucket to a modern concrete bowl. Pots come in all sizes as well as materials ranging from clay and ceramic to fibreglass and wood. The one feature they all must have is a hole in the bottom for drainage. If you need to make a hole, use a powerful electric drill or get a professional to do it for you.

Perennials need pots at least 12 inches (30 centimetres) in diameter; 20 inches (50 centimetres) is even better. Pots for shrubs such as boxwood or yew should be a minimum of 18 inches (45 centimetres) in diameter and at least 2 feet (60 centimetres) deep. To improve their chances of winter survival, line the container with sheets of Styrofoam for insulation. Annuals can be planted in almost any sized pot. Just make sure the plant enhances the style of container.

This gardener has oodles of taste and shows it in this selection of containers. Some have only one plant such as phormium (rear) and others have a combination of potato vines in black and gold (*Ipomoea* 'Blackie' and 'Marguerite'). Having a simple palette such as this can have a much more dramatic impact than one huge pot filled with fussy plants. It will, however, require daily watering. And make sure you use Soil Sponge or another product that holds in water. Put it near the roots, not the top of the plant.

Cover the hole at the bottom of the pot with a piece of landscape cloth (a black, water-permeable fabric sold as a weed barrier), a shard from a broken clay pot or a layer of sticks to stop the soil from running out with the water. If you have a very large pot, you can fill the bottom third with Styrofoam peanuts, or the leftover plastic six-pack containers that annuals usually come in turned upside down. This will enhance drainage and make the pot lighter. Never use garden soil in containers. Use potting mixes specially made for container growing: these are water-retentive mixes, many of which include slow-release fertilizer.

Fill the pot with moist potting mix to 2 inches (5 centimetres) below the lip of the pot. Set the plants in a pleasing arrangement; then plant them one at a time filling soil around them so the final soil level is about 1-2 inches (4 centimetres) below the lip. Don't jam too many plants in a container, and always combine plants that have the same light and water requirements. Water thoroughly. Most containers need watering daily (sometimes twice if they are exposed to a lot of sun and wind), and for long enough that water runs out of the bottom. That's when you know that the soil is moist through and through. If the potting mix has no fertilizer in it, add a fish fertilizer diluted at half strength every two or three weeks during the summer.

Under the Willow Tree

A weeping willow is the most discouraging plant to garden under but it can be done. Make sure you are adding enough water for your own plants and the tree nearby. Never plant so that you are interfering with the feeder roots. Start out with small plants and baby them along with compost and lots of water until they are well established on their own.

Under a Tree

We often want to fill the space under a large tree with plants. Some trees such as silver maple, willow, oak, honey locust and Kentucky coffee tree are not too bothered. Magnolias, pines, sugar maples and beeches are another matter; they have fleshy or extensive roots very close to the surface so they can suffer from the disturbance and also offer a lot of competition for the new plants.

If you want to get rid of lawn around trees to gain planting space, never use herbicides. Use sheet mulching (see page 43). If you do this over winter, you'll be able to plant in loose wonderful soil in spring.

Stick to small plants and dig only their planting holes (don't try to dig up the whole area). Don't put plants any closer than a foot (30 centimetres) away from the flare of the tree trunk. Add lots of mulch and water weekly in the first year. Every year, add 2 to 3 inches (5 to 8 centimetres) of organic mulch over the area under the tree.

Propping Up the Garden

If you have a combination of plants with varying heights, they will usually support each other. But some plants are inclined to lean or flop about unattractively. The time to deal with this is at planting time or soon after. Once plants have flopped, it's difficult to get them back up and looking decent.

Put in a sturdy wooden stake when planting tall perennials such as delphiniums and Oriental lilies, leaving about 6 inches (15 centimetres) of space between plant and stake. Tie the stem to the stake in a loose figure-eight with green vinyl garden tape, or loops cut from old pantyhose. Some late-blooming perennials, such as asters and phlox, can be pinched back in summer to make them sturdier. Get a supply of bamboo stakes painted green from the nursery—they become invisible in the garden. Put five or six stakes in a circle around any floppy clumps of plants and make a grid with string looped from stake to stake. The plant will grow up through the grid and eventually hide the whole support. Twiggy branches can also be inserted around a perennial to create a rough framework that the plant will also grow through and conceal. Finally, a simple and very useful support is that good old standby the tomato cage, which can hold up lots more than tomatoes.

"Plants have a powerful urge to live."

Propping up the garden with an extraordinary obelisk or another form of screen or riser should be done in selected parts of the garden to add another layer of interest. The style is very important. Make it fit with the kinds of plants you want nearby. In this case vibrant hollyhocks and purple coneflowers around the wooden obelisk look just right. Usually you would have vines crawling all over, but in this case the structure itself is the focal point.

Essential Planting Tips

Heed these tips and the planting guide that follows for success.

1. Always read the plant tag carefully to make sure you are putting the plant in the right light and soil conditions and allowing it sufficient room to grow.
2. Never put a plant in the ground with a dry root ball or desiccated roots; soak them well beforehand.
3. Cut off any broken stems or branches on woody plants and perennials, and trim any mushy or damaged roots from bare-root plants.
4. Plant in the early morning or late afternoon when it's cool, never at midday, and resist planting if a heat wave is expected.
5. Water new plants well at planting time. Let the hose dribble on all sides of the plant, so the root system and soil around it are thoroughly soaked.
6. Mulch as quickly as possible.

You'll get a feel for planting once you've had a few dozen plants in your hands during your first big planting blitz. Any fear of placing them improperly is usually overcome after you've put in a tree or two and moved a few perennials. Plants have a powerful urge to live and will usually survive some initial clumsiness, especially if you have paid attention to your soil. All that remains now is to learn what you need to do to keep them happy and thriving.

Garden Care

Garden
Organically
Fertilize
Know Birds
and Bugs
Weed
Water

Maintain
Fountains
Watch Your Edges
Deadhead
Prune
Divide Perennials
Seasonal Rituals
Troubleshooting

Garden Care

A pair of secateurs or tiny Japanese scissors will help you to keep your plants deadheaded properly. To maintain a garden well you need good tools kept very clean and stored properly. Plants need nipping away at on a regular basis, so view this as one of the most relaxing things you can do.

GOOD MAINTENANCE IS AT THE HEART OF A HEALTHY GARDEN—and great gardening. You can sense immediately when a garden is well cared for, it feels loved the minute you walk into it. That takes work.

Gardening isn't supposed to be easy, it's supposed to be stimulating for body and mind as well as being good for the soul. There is no such thing as a no-maintenance garden; even a low-maintenance one requires effort and certainly imagination. If you start out practising good management, just like learning the botanical names that soon trip off the tongue, it quickly becomes second nature. Keeping a garden journal, whether a plain notebook or a specially designed one, is a surprisingly helpful tool. Immediately get into the habit of taking pictures to keep track of what's gone into the garden and what's going on in the garden, and be sure to record the weather each day.

Observation is one of your best garden tools: you should be looking with a critical eye at the garden every day, not just assessing your design but keeping an eye out for things that need doing. Take action early and big problems are prevented. See a few aphids on a rose stem, immediately swish them off with a spray of the hose. If the garden starts to look unruly, you know there are plants that need pruning; when plants droop, they need watering. It's all too easy for the eye to adjust to things. When I first started gardening, I had a perfectly gorgeous shrub. It was several years old when I noticed a weed tree growing through the middle of it. Well, the weed tree had to have been growing for years but I'd adjusted to seeing it as one more branch. The tree was removed and the shrub survived, but I felt thoroughly chastened. Although plants do have strong survival skills, it is our job as gardeners to give them a hand. Here are the best ways to make sure your garden thrives.

Garden Organically

In addition to being an observant gardener, you must become an organic gardener. This is not a casual suggestion. The organic gardener recycles all the material that comes out of the garden (via composting and mulching) and is not dependent on chemical fertilizers and pesticides. Organic gardening is maintaining a garden using simple natural

Get to know good bugs (like the ladybug, above left) from the bad bugs by buying a handbook with clear pictures. Plant to encourage good bugs and they will help you create a healthy garden. It's also a good idea to remove weeds (above right) in early spring when the ground is moist, then again before they go to seed later in the season.

processes and is much less complicated than buying, measuring and applying chemicals. It is also healthier for the plants, for the insects and for you.

Fertilize

All you need to fertilize your plants is a combination of manure and compost. Just place a layer an inch (2.5 centimetres) deep around the plant and water it in. Or make a batch of compost tea: Put a bag (half an old pillowcase works well) of compost in a large bucket of water and let it steep for a week. Take out the bag and put the resulting "tea" in bottles. Spray the plants top to bottom with about 1/2 cup (125 millilitres) of compost tea diluted in 2 cups (500 millilitres) of water. They'll love it.

Know Your Birds and Bugs

Learn to tell the difference between good bugs and bad (bad, that is, according to gardeners who don't want their plants chewed or destroyed). Get a child's book of bugs—it will give you all the information you need— and memorize it (see bibliography, page 170). If you install a wide variety of plants, you'll attract such good bugs as ladybugs, spiders and ground beetles. They in turn will bump off the detrimental ones such as aphids, slugs and caterpillars.

Weeds such as ox eye daisy (above left) and butterfly weed (above right), with their vibrant blooms, can be mistaken for benevolent flowers, but can be wildly invasive if they get out of your control.

Birds are another major form of pest control, gobbling all sorts of caterpillars and insect eggs. Attract birds to your garden by providing feeders, water sources and nesting sites. Insect problems are better solved by letting nature take care of its own than by using chemical pesticides whose full impact we can't know.

That said, one all-round safe treatment for pests such as aphids is one teaspoon (5 millilitres) of liquid soap in 4 cups (1 litre) of water. Spray this over the tender tips and leaves (both sides) of the affected plant. Or blast the pests off with a steady stream of water from the hose. To deal with slugs, hand-picking and squishing them underfoot is the most reliable method if you aren't squeamish. But attracting them to a boozy death the old-fashioned way, with margarine or yogurt containers of beer, works too. Drawn to the beer, they fall in and drown. Encourage toads to your garden by providing water (a pond or stream), shady retreats and lots of mulch: a single toad can eat ten thousand slugs and other delicacies in one season.

Weed

A weed is often referred to as a plant out of place. You probably are familiar with dandelions and crabgrass in lawns; as you garden you will learn to recognize common weeds such as lamb's quarters, purslane, chickweed and thistles. Weeds are opportunistic and aggressive and will

knock off vulnerable plants by stealing nutrients and sunlight. Try to get rid of them when they are still small and definitely get them before they go to seed. As the saying goes, "A year of seeding means seven years weeding." In spring, if you are unsure whether seedlings are weeds or not, let them grow bigger and more recognizable. Get into the habit of weeding on a weekly basis as you make your rounds of the garden. You can winkle out weeds easily when the ground is moist. Use a weeding tool or even an old screwdriver and be sure to get the whole root system. If they have no seeds, toss them into the composter. Any weeds with seeds should be put in the garbage.

Water

It's not necessary to have a complex watering system. An ordinary hose with a nozzle will work very efficiently. Watering isn't a science but it is an art that requires a good eye, and overwatering is as bad as underwatering. I usually have one plant with huge leaves such as an umbrella plant (*Darmera peltata*) in each border; when that plant starts to droop, I know it's time to get out the hose. Another way to tell if it's time to water is to push your fingers into the soil; if it's still dry at the second knuckle, it needs water.

If you have a sprinkler, set it on a ladder to raise it off the ground and deliver water to a much larger area like a gentle rain. Do this in the early morning so the water on the leaves has a chance to evaporate over the course of the day; wet foliage can lead to disease. When using a watering can, fill it and let it sit for at least twenty minutes before

Before watering, let water sit in a container until it reaches room temperature or collect it in a rain butt attached to a downspout from the eaves. This is the best water for any plant.

pouring the water on your plants. This allows the chlorine in tap water to evaporate and also helps to warm the water slightly, which is easier on the plants (though they will certainly make do with the cold water from the hose). Watering perennials and annuals by hand at the soil level gets the water to the root zone and avoids getting the leaves wet. For trees and shrubs, leave the hose gently dribbling on the ground for an hour or so near each plant—this lets the water percolate slowly and deeply into the soil. Another option is to lay soaker hoses through your beds; this type of hose, usually made of rubber, has tiny holes along its length that allow the water to seep out slowly.

Maintain Fountains and Birdbaths

Water in birdbaths must be changed every couple of days and the basin scrubbed out regularly to prevent algae buildup and to reduce the chance of West Nile virus (see page 55). Fountains can be treated with algicides to keep the water clear but they will still need topping up and a complete water change occasionally. Before winter, remove the pump, clean it and store it. Then thoroughly clean the fountain and store it in a shed if it won't withstand winter outdoors.

Watch Your Edges

Clean crisp edges to lawns and borders not only outline your design but also make a garden look extremely well cared for. To maintain a definite edge between lawn and flower bed, take a very sharp spade and cut the turf downward at a slight outward angle. Take out any turf trimmings and push the soil up on to the flower bed, creating a V-shaped trough between turf and flower bed. Continue this all the way along the edge of the lawn. For a more permanent solution, you can make hard edges of bricks, stones, railway ties, metal or poured concrete.

Deadhead

I find the most relaxing chore in the garden is deadheading—removing the spent flower heads. When everything seems a bit blowsy and tattered, it's the controlling hand that keeps the garden looking lively and, I hate to admit, clean and tidy. Deadheading promotes longer blooming because with the dead flowers gone seeds can't form, so the plant keeps blooming in a mad effort to produce more. This is especially true of annuals, but many perennials will have a second flush of flowers as well. Deadhead regularly—two or three times a week—and see what a

Proper pruning techniques can be learned. The first rule is don't leave nasty stubs to attract bugs and disease. Use a sharp instrument and make sure it's far enough from the stem to allow a collar to grow, but not too flat against the trunk or stem to cause damage.

difference it makes. I go out in the cool of the day and always travel through the garden with something sharp in my hands ready for a little creative snipping.

Secateurs or the special tiny Japanese scissors are terrific for this job. Make sure they are clean: use a smooth cloth with some denatured alcohol on it and wipe the blades after deadheading each plant. For many annuals, you can just nip the old flowers off with your fingertips. Flowers that bloom on long stems, such as hostas, should have the whole stem taken down to about an inch (2.5 centimetres) or so. Bushy plants with lots of small flowers, such as threadleaf coreopsis, would take forever to deadhead individually. Get out the garden shears and give the whole plant a good haircut; it will respond with another round of flowers.

Prune

Pruning—the careful cutting back of stems and branches of plants, especially woody plants—is done to keep a tree or shrub healthy, maintain a good shape, improve flowering and fruiting and give you a little control. But this vital part of any annual maintenance program is where many people go off the deep end. Done badly, pruning does more harm than good; done well, it will enhance the whole garden. Pruning should not be done simply to control the size of a plant—for example, to keep it below your windows. If you need to do that, consider moving the plant to a more suitable spot and replacing it with something that will grow naturally to the desired height.

Pruning Trees

Check your trees every year, but realize that not every single one will need annual pruning. When you see wayward or dead branches inside the canopy, you'll know it's time to act. Pruning trees is often better left to the experts—a good arbourist can be your garden's best friend. But you should still know what to look for: anyone who wants to climb your tree using spikes on his boots is not a pro. This will damage the tree. Good guys use ropes and haul themselves around in the most terrifying and impossible ways.

Branches should be cut back smoothly to the slight swelling at their base (called the branch collar) without tearing the bark. The cuts should not be flush with the trunk nor leave long stubs. No goo or paint should be applied to the wounds; trees will heal on their own. Most trees can be pruned in late winter or in early spring but some, such as birches and maples, should be left until summer. They will lose too much sap if pruned early, weakening them and making them vulnerable to diseases.

Pruning Shrubs

Most shrubs benefit from annual pruning to maintain their health and beauty. Good pruning gets rid of dead or diseased wood, brings light and air into the centre of the plant, promotes new growth and flowering, and gives the shrub a handsome shape on an excellent framework. Autumn-flowering shrubs should be pruned in spring. Spring-flowering shrubs should be pruned only after they have finished blooming. One note of caution: don't cut back the old stems of silver-leafed plants such as artemisia, caryopteris, lavender and Russian sage in spring until you see lots of new growth at the base.

It's often recommended that you cut out one-third of a shrub every year in a constant renewal process. But this does not mean shearing back the plant by a third. It means removing one-third of the oldest stems right down to the base. Do this every year for three years and you'll have a totally rejuvenated plant. If you have a small spindly shrub with just a few stems, you can cut them back by as much as half. This will force the production of new shoots. Then, the following year, you

On Arbourists

Getting a certified arbourist into the garden will be a good investment. Have the arbourist come in every two years once you've got your garden in good shape. Watch the arbourist's work very carefully, ask lots of questions, check out what equipment they use (small stuff like secateurs and loppers) and try to imitate what they do.

can proceed with regular pruning. Some shrubs such as lilacs and cherry trees produce shoots from the base—these are called suckers. It's a good idea to cut suckers back to ground level to keep the mother plant strong. You can do this any time, but spring is best.

Pruning can be light (removing the obvious dead, awkward or really old stems) or hard (more severe chopping). For instance: To promote the vivid new growth on shrubs such as elders, purple smoke bush and shrubby dogwoods, cut them back severely to 6 or 8 inches (15 or 20 centimetres) from the ground in early spring. A drastic form of rejuvenation is coppicing; this involves cutting back an unruly shrub entirely to 4 or 5 inches (10 or 12.5 centimetres) from the ground. Once the shrub resprouts, you can pinch back the stems to encourage bushiness and then implement a regular pruning program to maintain its form.

When you tackle a pruning job, clean up the area around the shrub so you have a clear view and easy access. Make sure you have sharp, clean secateurs and loppers. Remove any dead branches or those that are crossing (they will chafe each other and cause wounds), then proceed with the removal of the oldest stems. When pruning for shape, do it gradually, stepping back after every cut to check on the overall look. Remember that you are enhancing the shrub's natural growth habit, not forcing it into an unnatural form. One of the smartest

When pruning a shrub, take out all dead material and crossing branches in early spring (above opposite left). Remove suckers at ground level (above opposite right). Pruning wisteria (above left) will help ensure it will bloom. Cut back to two buds in spring (above right), keeping the shape of the vines; then in summer cut back again. Watch for flower buds though and don't touch them.

suggestions I've ever read was made by the great English garden designer Russell Page, who advised that if you lie down under a shrub or small tree and look upward, you will understand its architecture.

Pruning Vines

Any vigorous vines that threaten to get into the soffits of your roof, cover your windows or strangle the mail carrier should be whacked right back to manageable size, but most vines just need any dead material cleaned out in early spring. Three vines with more specific pruning requirements are:

CLEMATIS: Spring-flowering clematis can have any overly tangled growth removed after they've bloomed, or they can be left alone to cover a fence or arbour. Any large-flowered hybrids such as 'Henryi', 'Ramona' and 'Nelly Moser' that bloom in early summer should be cut back in early spring to the first pair of really large strong buds. The late-blooming forms (including *C. viticella*, the 'Jackmanii' hybrids and sweet autumn clematis) can be chopped back to about a foot (30 centimetres) from the ground in spring.

CLIMBING HYDRANGEA (*Hydrangea petiolaris*): After it has flowered, prune back the branches with the spent flowers and any other errant shoots to a strong leaf bud. Once it gets established, climbing hydrangea is a very

"You will often hear that peonies don't like being divided. Well, they aren't that fussy and divide up very nicely in autumn."

vigorous plant with thick woody stems, so prune it every year to keep it from getting too big and heavy.

WISTERIA: Give it a hard pruning twice a year to keep it under control and promote blooming. In late winter or early spring (before it leafs out), prune off everything except the main stem and framework branches (these are the branches that give it its structure). In midsummer in your area, tackle all the wild new growth, cutting each branch back severely to three or four buds from the main stems.

Divide Perennials

Many perennials benefit from being divided every two to three years. The plants give you a pretty good idea when they need dividing by developing big bare patches in the centre, or getting too large for the space they're in (irises, grasses and hostas are the biggest offenders). Dividing means digging up the whole plant, roots and all, and literally pulling it apart with your fingers or cutting it vertically into pieces with a very sharp knife or spade. Plants with fleshy, knotted root systems such as daylilies can be pried apart with two garden forks. Each of these pieces (called divisions) should have some top growth and roots. They can then be planted like any perennial (or potted and given away to friends). If you can't plant the divisions right away, cover them with a damp cloth until you are ready, but only for a day or so. Dividing your plants not only keeps them healthy but is also an excellent way of expanding your plantings for free.

The optimum time to divide plants (especially ornamental grasses and late-season bloomers) is in early spring when the new growth is starting. Plants are so full of growth hormones at this time they will hardly look back.

If you must divide perennials later in summer when they're in full leaf or in bloom, be aware that they will look really sad for a while, but with plenty of water, they will eventually perk up. Perennials such as coral bells, catmint, bellflowers and hardy salvias can be divided in fall, but make sure the divisions have plenty of roots and plant them at least

Far right: Dividing perennials will not only keep them healthy, it will mean you've got plants to spread around or share. Use a clean shovel and a large bread knife or a small saw to divide up the big ones. Clumps of plants the size of these foxgloves are just about ready to be divided up once they've finished blooming.

six to eight weeks before you expect a hard frost so they have time to get established before winter.

You will often hear that peonies don't like being divided. Well, they aren't that fussy and divide up very nicely in autumn. Simply dig up the plant as the foliage starts to go yellow. Cut back the leaves and hose the soil off the root ball. This helps you to see where the "eyes" are located: the eyes are the bumps on the root where buds develop. Chop the root system into pieces, making sure that each division has at least three eyes on it. Plant the divisions just as you would plant peonies (see page 131) making sure they are planted shallowly. This is one time when you can use soil enriched with compost and manure to fill the hole rather than just top-dress. Be sure they are watered well. Other perennials that have eyes include bleeding heart and Virginia bluebells; handle divisions of these carefully so you don't damage the eyes.

Seasonal Rituals

Every season brings its own rituals and jobs to perform. Some are less obvious than others, so here is an outline of what you should be doing. And while you're out there, absorb the smells and sights in your garden— this form of meditation is as important for your soul as working in the garden is for your body.

Spring

Being a slave to garden housekeeping is relevant only one time of the year and that's spring.

Clean up all the tools you left lying about dirty last autumn. You should never go into the garden with dirty tools because it's possible to carry disease through the garden that way. A good scrubbing in hot soapy water will do for shovels and trowels; try a mixture of a little sand and vegetable oil to clean up secateurs.

In early spring, scrape away any old mulch from last fall and throw it into the composter to continue breaking down. The soil will warm up more quickly without its mulch blanket. Don't worry if there's one more snowstorm, the plants are used to it.

Cast an eye over your conifers; cut off winter-killed dead branches and, wearing rubber or leather gloves, rub any brown needles off the rest of the plant. Cut off any dieback on roses: this is usually the ends of the branches that have died over winter; dieback will look brown, the live part of the branches or canes will look greener. Pull back the mulch,

This is one of the loveliest gardens I've been in. Great care has been taken to make sure the garden looks perfect from every window in every season. The bones of the garden in winter (bottom right) expose its superb underpinnings. This is the harmony all gardeners want to achieve and it takes vision and thoughtfulness and an eye to the future.

"Summer is a time for puttering in the garden."

plant a clove of garlic beside each rose bush to help keep fungal diseases and pests at bay, sprinkle a handful of Epsom salts around them to give the soil a potassium boost, and replace the mulch. Pick or cut off any yucky leaves from perennials that weren't cleaned up last fall, and whack back ornamental grasses to about 3 inches (8 centimetres) so the sun will warm up the middle of the clump and prompt new growth. It takes two or three weeks for new growth to appear so don't be discouraged and think you've killed them off.

Check the compost and even if it isn't perfectly finished (that is, everything has broken down to a crumbly, brown soil-like humus), mix it up with manure and chopped-up leaves for spring mulch.

Once the soil is warm and plants start to show new growth, put down a layer of spring mulch 2 inches (5 centimetres) deep. Rain or melting snow will easily percolate through this carpet. If rain is scarce, don't hesitate to check the soil and get the hose out and water. We hope for delicious spring rains but they don't always happen.

Summer

Summer is a time for puttering in the garden—deadheading, watering containers, keeping on top of the weeds, tucking in a few new plants wherever there's a spot, inhaling the scents and drinking in the sights. With the garden in full flush, it's also the best time to get ideas about where to move things. For instance, you might see two plants with gorgeous pink blooms in different areas of the garden; well, think about putting them closer together in autumn or next spring. Take pictures, date them and stick them in your journal so you will remember that brilliant idea when the time comes. It's amazing how quickly you forget where things are once winter arrives.

Another summer task is pinching back, which means cutting back a plant's growing tips. It's done for a couple of reasons. First, many of the big stars of autumn—asters, chrysanthemums, heliopsis, goldenrod and boltonia—tend to get so tall they either fall over or look out of scale in the garden. To prevent this, pinch back about a third of the newest growth around the end of July. This will make the remaining stems

sturdier and the plant less inclined to flop over. Pinching back a young plant will also make it bushier. When the plant has reached 4 to 5 inches (10 to 12.5 centimetres) in height, nip back the ends and any buds, keeping a rounded form. Use little Japanese scissors to get a good sharp cut. Each pinched-back branch will put out several new branches.

Autumn

With shorter days and falling temperatures, plants start heading toward dormancy, and there is a temptation to put the garden to bed. Urban philosopher L. Rust Hills once said: "Tidying as you go is half the fun." He was not, however, a gardener. You can tidy up the autumnal garden far too much. Don't be too scrupulous or you'll disturb the natural processes. Leave anything in bloom (roses, asters, late viburnums) or that has useful seed heads (food for birds) or that will be beautiful later on (vines over a fence resembling posh draperies, grasses waving in the breeze). Ultimately, these elements will combine to provide a transcendent winter scene.

You can remove soggy brown leaves from perennials such as peonies, hostas, daylilies and irises. Mushy foliage will attract slugs and sowbugs and give them a great place to overwinter. Toss these leaves into the composter. If you have wormwood (*Artemisia absinthium*), chop off some of the leaves and steep them in water: pour this tea around hostas to discourage slugs from overwintering in them.

Remove any recognizable weeds from the garden before the soil freezes, and mow the lawn for the last time (give it a sprinkle of organic fertilizer now for quick greening-up come spring). Make sure any new plants and all trees and evergreens are deeply watered before the ground freezes. Evergreens lose water through their needles and leaves all winter and need to have plenty in reserve in their roots. A slow drizzle from the hose moved all around the plant works best. Once everything is well-watered, drain your hoses and put them away. Don't forget to clean up your tools—if you have good equipment, it pays to look after it. Rub secateurs, shovels and trowels with the finest grade of steel wool and some vegetable oil to remove mud and accumulated rust.

Some annuals can be kept over winter. One way is to take cuttings, that is, snip pieces 3 to 4 inches (8 to 10 centimetres) long off the ends of the branches. Before the first frost, take cuttings from plants such as annual geraniums and coleus. Dip the cut ends into rooting hormone (you can buy it at any garden centre), stick them into small pots filled with moist potting soil and keep them in a bright spot indoors. Once they root, give them light, water and a bit of fertilizer over winter until you can plant them out next spring. Tender bulbous plants such as dahlias, cannas and tuberous begonias can also be stored over winter. Dig them up, cut off the tops, shake the soil off them, roll them in fungicide (again, you can get this at your local garden centre) and store them in a medium such as kitty litter, sawdust or vermiculite in a cool dark spot such as a basement or heated garage.

When it comes to containers, don't leave ceramic or terra-cotta pots outside where they will get wet and then crack or shatter; empty them out and wash thoroughly, then stack with sections of newspaper in between them and store in a garage or shed. If you have plants in frost-proof pots (fibreglass, for example, lined with Styrofoam) designed to be left outdoors, make sure they are raised off the ground on bricks or L-shaped pieces of clay called chocks or pot feet. Keep a couple of favourite pots that you can fill with brightly coloured twigs, evergreen branches and berries to put by the front door or near a window.

If you have roses that aren't especially hardy in your zone, protect them by encircling the base of the plant with a generous ring of chicken wire and filling it with leaves or soil. This process is called hilling up (note that the plants have to be hilled down in spring). Don't cut back roses in fall; just tack any floppy canes of climbing roses to their supports. Small new trees and evergreens can often benefit from some protection from drying winds and southern sun in their first year. You can wrap them loosely, like draping fabric over a mannequin, in a light insulation cloth or burlap (available at your local garden centre). If you have a new tree with fragile buds (a magnolia, for instance), place tall bamboo stakes around the tree and wrap insulation cloth and burlap around the stakes, stapling it in place to create a doubly protective screen. Finally, don't forget to put down a layer of winter mulch once there is hard frost in the ground.

Winter

This is the time for creative revisualizing of the garden for next year. Winter reveals the bones of the garden—all the structure you have built

The tranquility of winter is captured in this beautifully structured garden. Nothing has been cut back too far, leaving plant shadows on the snow and seeds and berries for birds. It's a good time to look for winter arrangements, so take a few bits from artemisias, dogwoods with different coloured bark, as well as some evergreens. The garden never stops working for a good gardener.

into it. If you have done a good job, it will be looking absolutely gorgeous. If not, make notes about what improvements you can make in spring. Are there areas which would be perked up with an additional evergreen or two? Are there enough shrubs with stems of red, yellow and citrus green to animate the scene? Do you have plenty of plants with berries and ornamental grasses with lovely plumes?

If you have a heavy snowfall that bends and flattens the plants, go out with a ski or broom to knock the snow off the grasses. Brush the snow gently off the shrubs so they don't split under the weight. If you have an ice storm, though, leave them be; you can do more harm than good whacking frozen ice-coated branches.

Troubleshooting

When things look to be going wrong, try to determine the root cause and whether it is a temporary glitch or more permanent affliction. For instance, if your lawn goes brown in a hot dry summer, don't worry. It has just gone into dormancy and will green up once it gets enough rain. Most problems can be traced to issues with soil, water or light. If a shrub or perennial blooms one year and not the next, chances are it is too shaded and needs moving to a sunnier spot. If plants are drooping,

Pest Control

A healthy spritz of homemade bugkiller (some soap in a container of water), even a hard spray with the hose will get rid of most pests. Compost tea is always a great thing: put a cup of compost into an old sack or pillowcase and leave it in a bucket of water for a week. Dilute it 10 to one with water and spread it around. Your plants will love you.

check to see if they have too little or too much water. If all or part of a tree such as redbud or Japanese maple suddenly dies back, you may have a fungal disease called verticillium wilt in your soil. It's not easily treated so the best solution is to take the plant out and put in a tree that is more wilt-resistant and use a lot of compost in that area.

Sickly-looking plants (discoloured leaves, spindly stems) may indicate that your soil is lacking nutrients. For example, yellow older leaves and poor growth are signs of nitrogen deficiency; stunted plants and bronzing leaves show a shortage of phosphorus; and leaves with brown edges and yellow spots indicate lack of potassium. The solution is to beef up your composting program.

If you see damaging insects (aphids, slugs, caterpillars, etc.), try the solutions described on page 145. The problem will usually correct itself. For insect infestations of trees, indicated by holes in the bark and obviously dying branches, however, call in an arbourist for a diagnosis. Always cut out any dead or diseased branches from trees and shrubs. This is the first line of defence. If in doubt, take a branch or leaf of the problem plant to your local garden centre and see if they can tell you the cause.

Gardening is one of the most fascinating and compelling projects you can throw yourself into. It's fascinating intellectually and compelling to research. It is a way of staying connected with the world around you, and a way of having control over your environment. If we should leave the planet in better condition than we found it, then gardening is one small local solution. Going slowly through the seven steps suggested here is just the beginning of what can become an obsession. Don't despair if your garden doesn't look exactly as you imagined it this year. There is always the dream, hope and intention that it will be better next year. More than any other art form, a garden takes time to come into perfection.

Gardeners are always rethinking. And every few years some of us decide it's time to "re-vision" the garden, pull things out, move them around, add new structures. Tinkering mentally with what you've done, spending the winter thinking about the garden, drawing up those

"Gardening is one of the most fascinating and compelling projects you can throw yourself into."

impossible dream lists, finding the plants and seeing them suddenly and exquisitely mesh together are all part of this wonderful way of living. The best thing of all is that a garden is never finished, it's always in the realm of possibility.

Top Tips for Garden Maintenance

1. It doesn't matter how big or small the garden, get a composter and you'll have both mulch and fertilizer for free.
2. Underwatering is bad, and so is overwatering—learn to recognize when to water and how.
3. Gardening organically rather than using a lot of pesticides is cheaper and much less confusing than loading on the chemicals.
4. Learn about and improve your soil.
5. Deadhead to keep annuals and perennials blooming and looking good until autumn.
6. Prune shrubs and trees for shape and form, but not after the middle of August.
7. Keep borders and lawns neatly edged; it brings instant order to the garden.
8. Mulch, mulch, mulch.

Appendix:
The Indispensable Plant List

This selection of wonderful plants will help you get started. I have included lots of perennials because I think they contribute a great deal to a garden.

Most annuals bloom all summer until frost kills them. All plants listed here prefer full sun unless specified otherwise.

Selecting Plants for Colour
(see page 93)

Blue/purple

SHRUBS

CARYOPTERIS (*Caryopteris* x *clandonensis* 'Kew Blue'). Structural plant; blooms in late summer. H: 3 ft. (90 cm).

PERENNIALS

BELLFLOWER
(*Campanula carpatica* 'Blue Clips'). Large bell-shaped flowers in summer. H: 9 in. (22 cm).
(*C. glomerata*). Deep purple/blue blooms in summer. H: 18 in. (45 cm).
(*C. latifolia*). Tubular bell-shaped flowers in summer. H: 4 ft. (1.2 m).
FLAX (*Linum perenne*). Fine-textured foliage; small flowers in early summer; long-blooming. H: 2 ft. (60 cm).
MONKSHOOD (*Aconitum* spp.). Poisonous; blooms in late summer; attracts bumblebees; needs rich soil in part shade. H: 2 to 5 ft. (60 cm to 1.5 m).
RUSSIAN SAGE (*Perovskia atriplicifolia*). Silver foliage; blooms in summer. H: 4 ft. (1.2 m).
SALVIA
(*S.* x *sylvestris* 'May Night'). Blooms in early summer. H: 28 in. (70 cm).
(*S. verticillata* 'Purple Rain'). Grey-purple blooms in early summer. H: 20 in. (50 cm).

ANNUALS

SALVIA (*Salvia guaranitica* 'Blue Enigma'). Large blooms on strong stems. H: 4 ft. (1.2 m).

Gold

SHRUBS

BARBERRY (*Berberis thunbergii* 'Sunsation'). Slow-growing; mounded form; brilliant yellow leaves. H: 3 to 4 ft. (90 cm to 1.2 m).
FULL-MOON JAPANESE MAPLE (*Acer shirasawanum* 'Aureum'). Elegant branching pattern; hardy to -23°C (-9°F); intense gold foliage in fall; takes dappled shade. H: 20 ft. (6 m).
GOLDEN SMOKE BUSH (*Cotinus coggygria* 'Golden Spirit'). Chartreuse foliage; superb with purple sedums. H: 6 ft. (1.8 m).
NINEBARK (*Physocarpus opulifolius* 'Dart's Gold'). Ideal substitute for forsythia in colder areas. H: 5 ft. (1.5 m).
VARIEGATED DOGWOOD (*Cornus alba* 'Aurea'). Leaves suffused with yellow; striking red stems. H: 7 ft. (2.1 m).

PERENNIALS

BOWLES' GOLDEN SEDGE (*Carex elata* 'Aurea'). Upright form; yellow blades with green edges; likes moist soil in shade. H: 20 in. (50 cm).
CORALBELLS (*Heuchera* 'Marmalade'). Peachy bronze foliage; brownish flowers in spring; useful filler, edger or container plant; needs part shade. H: 10 to 16 in. (25 to 40 cm).
HOSTA
All like part shade to shade.
(*H.* 'Amber Tiara'). Thick golden leaves; dark purple blooms in midsummer. H: 15 in. (38 cm).
(*H.* 'Gold Standard'). Golden leaves edged in green; lavender flowers in summer. H: 30 in. (75 cm).
(*H.* 'Golden Tusk'). Thick yellow leaves; near white flowers in summer. H: 22 in. (55 cm).
(*H.* 'Guacamole'). Chartreuse leaves; fragrant white flowers in late summer. H: 2 ft. (60 cm).
(*H.* 'Little Sunspot'). Heart-shaped leaves with green edge; pale lavender flowers in summer. H: 6 in. (15 cm).
(*H.* 'Stained Glass'). Brilliant gold leaves with green veins; fragrant lavender flowers in late summer. H: 15 in. (38 cm).
(*H.* 'Sum and Substance'). Huge puckered greeny gold leaves; pale lavender flowers in late summer. H: 3 ft. (90 cm).
(*H.* 'Sun Power'). Upright habit; lavender flowers in early summer. H: 2 ft. (60 cm).
JAPANESE FOREST GRASS (*Hakonechloa macra* 'All Gold'). Strong golden foliage; cascading form. Takes sun or shade. H: 10 in. (25 cm).
PERENNIAL BACHELOR'S BUTTONS (*Centaurea montana* 'Gold Bullion'). Bright yellow leaves; brilliant blue cornflower blooms in early summer. H: 15 in. (38 cm).
Sedum (*Sedum* 'Angelina'). Needle-shaped foliage. H: 6 in. (15 cm).
TOAD LILY
(*Tricyrtis hirta* 'Golden Gleam'). Chartreuse leaves; orchid-like flowers in autumn; part shade to shade. H: 3 ft. (90 cm).
(*T. h.* 'Gold Leaf'). Needs morning sun to enhance leaf

colour; purple spotted blooms in late summer; part shade. H: 2 ft. (60 cm).

Burgundy

TREES/SHRUBS

EASTERN REDBUD (*Cercis canadensis* 'Forest Pansy'). Superb heart-shaped, red-purple leaves; dark pink flowers in spring; late to leaf out. H: 30 ft. (10 m).

NINEBARK (*Physocarpus opulifolius* 'Diabolo'). Intense maroon foliage; pink-tinged white blooms in spring. H: 10 ft. (3 m).

PURPLE SMOKE BUSH (*Cotinus coggygria*). Frothy "smoky" blooms in summer; good fall colour. H: 15 ft. (4.5 m).

WEIGELA (*Weigela* 'Midnight Wine'). Tubular pink blooms in early summer attract hummingbirds. H: 2 ft. (60 cm).

PERENNIALS

CARDINAL FLOWER (*Lobelia* 'Russian Princess'). Velvety dark foliage; magenta-purple blooms in summer. H: 30 in. (75 cm).

EUPHORBIA (*Euphorbia dulcis* 'Chameleon'). Purple leaves; acid green flowers in spring; a prolific seeder. H: 2 ft. (60 cm).

SEDUM (*Sedum* x 'Mohrchen'). Fleshy maroon leaves; clear pink blooms in fall. H: 2 ft. (60 cm).

ANNUALS

COLEUS (*Solenostemon scutellarioides*). Foliage colours from lime to black; cultivars include 'Purple Emperor', 'Inky Fingers' and 'Black Dragon'; needs part shade. H: 12 to 18 in. (30 to 45 cm).

ORNAMENTAL MILLET (*Pennisetum glaucum* 'Purple Majesty'). Dramatic maroon, corn-like leaves. H: 6 ft. (1.8 m).

PURPLE FOUNTAIN GRASS (*Pennisetum setaceum* 'Rubrum'). Dark leaves and plumes; excellent in containers. H: 3 ft. (90 cm).

Orange

PERENNIALS

BUTTERFLY WEED (*Asclepias tuberosa*). Attracts butterflies; blooms in summer. H: 2 ft. (60 cm).

MALTESE CROSS (*Lychnis chalcedonica*). Brilliant rounded flower heads in early summer. H: 4 ft. (1.2 m).

NEW ZEALAND FLAX (*Phormium tenax* 'Sundowner'). Strappy green and orange leaves; good container plant. H: 4 to 6 ft. (1.2 to 1.8 m).

SNEEZEWEED (*Helenium* spp.). Vivid daisy-type flowers in summer. H: 2 to 5 ft. (60 cm to 1.5 m).

SPURGE (*Euphorbia griffithii* 'Fireglow'). Blue-green foliage; blooms in summer. H: 27 in. (70 cm).

ANNUALS

MARIGOLD (*Tagetes*). Bright hues; ferny foliage. H: 8 to 36 in. (20 to 90 cm).

Red

PERENNIALS

BEE BALM (*Monarda* 'Raspberry Wine'). Shaggy blooms all summer attract hummingbirds. H: 3 ft. (90 cm).

MONTBRETIA (*Crocosmia* 'Lucifer'). Showy tubular flowers in midsummer. H: 4 ft. (1.2 m).

ANNUALS

DAHLIA (*Dahlia* 'Bishop of Llandaff'). Vivid red blooms; near-black foliage. H: 4 ft. (1.2 m).

White

TREES

CAROLINA SILVER BELL (*Halesia carolina*). Native tree; bell-shaped flowers in spring; golden fall foliage; tolerates part shade. H: 25 ft. (7.5 m).

GIANT DOGWOOD (*C. controversa* 'Variegata'). Silver variegated leaves; white blooms in spring; tolerates part shade. H: 25 ft. (7.5 m).

JAPANESE SNOWBELL (*Styrax japonicus*). Horizontal branching pattern; dangling bells in late spring. H: 30 ft. (9 m).

PACIFIC DOGWOOD (*Cornus nuttallii*). Native tree; ecru blooms in spring; sun to part shade. H: 40 ft. (12 m).

PAGODA DOGWOOD (*Cornus alternifolia* 'Argentea'). Cream variegated foliage; blooms in spring; tolerates shade. H: 20 ft. (6 m).

SHRUBS

CINQUEFOIL (*Potentilla fruticosa* 'Abbotswood'). Trouble-free; blooms all summer. H: 3 ft. (1 m).

DOUBLEFILE VIBURNUM (*Viburnum plicatum f. tomentosum* 'Shasta'). Stunning spring flowers; wide horizontal form. H: 6 ft. (1.8 m).

FOTHERGILLA (*Fothergilla gardenii*). Scented bottlebrush flowers in spring; neon autumn foliage. H: 3 ft. (1 m).

PEARLBUSH (*Exochorda* x *macrantha* 'The Bride'). Blooms in spring/early summer. H: 6 ft. (1.8 m).

ROSE (*Rosa rugosa* 'Henry Hudson'). Fragrant blooms all summer; very hardy. H: 4 ft. (1.2 m).

STAR MAGNOLIA (*Magnolia stellata*). Pink-flushed flowers in spring; glossy leaves; attractive form. H: 10 ft. (3 m).

PERENNIALS

CANDYTUFT (*Iberis sempervirens*). Good edging plant; round clusters of blooms in spring. H: 1 ft. (30 cm).

CULVER'S ROOT (*Veronicastrum virginicum*). Native perennial; spires of blooms in midsummer; attracts insects. H: 5 ft. (1.5 m).

LILY
(*Lilium* 'Casa Blanca'). Highly scented flowers in midsummer. H: 4 ft. (1.2 m).
(*L.* 'White Horse'). Incandescent blooms in summer. H: 42 in. (105 cm).
Madonna lily (*L. candidum*). Heady scent; blooms in summer. H: 6 ft. (1.8 m).

ANNUALS

CLEOME (*Cleome* 'Helen Campbell'). Large round spiky flowers. H: 5 ft. (1.5 m).

FLOWERING TOBACCO (*Nicotiana sylvestris*). Scented flowers; huge leaves. H: 5 ft. (1.5 m).

Black

SHRUB

BLACK-LEAF ELDER
Sambucus 'Black Beauty'). Needs full sun to retain its black foliage; pink flower clusters in early summer. H: 6 to 10 ft. (1.8 to 3 m).
(S. 'Black Lace'). Deeply cut leaves; pink blooms in early summer. H: 6 ft. (1.8 m).

PERENNIALS

BLACK IRIS (*Iris chrysographes*). Velvety blooms with gold veins in early summer. H: 2 ft. (60 cm).

BLACK MONDO GRASS (*Ophiopogon planiscapus* 'Black Knight'). Spiky black foliage; small white flowers in summer and blue-black fruits. H: 6 in. (15 cm).

CORAL BELLS
(*Heuchera* 'Black Beauty'). Glossy leaves; white flowers in summer; tolerates part shade. H: 10 in. (25 cm).
(H. 'Obsidian'). Smooth rounded leaves; white flowers in summer; holds its colour well; takes shade. H: 10 in. (25 cm).

COW PARSLEY (*Anthriscus sylvestris* 'Ravenswing'). Fine texture; white flowers in summer; vigorous self-seeder. H: 3 ft. (90 cm).

DAYLILY
(*Hemerocallis* 'Ed Murray'). Long-lasting flowers in late

spring. H: 30 in. (75 cm).
(H. 'Jungle Beauty'). Blooms in midsummer. H: 30 in. (75 cm).

JAPANESE PARSLEY (*Cryptotaenia japonica* 'Atropurpurea'). Black-brown foliage; small white flowers in summer; vigorous self-seeder; tolerates part shade. H: 16 in. (40 cm).

Selecting Trees and Shrubs
(see page 100)

Evergreens

JAPANESE STONE PINE (*Pinus pumila* 'Dwarf Blue'). Wide horizontal spreading form; intense blue needles. H: 3 ft. (1.8 m).

JAPANESE UMBRELLA PINE (*Sciadopitys verticillata*). Whorls of glossy green needles. H: 30 ft. (9 m) in cultivation.

LODGEPOLE PINE (*Pinus contorta* 'Taylor's Sunburst'). Bright yellow new growth in spring. H: 15 ft. (4.5 m).

NORWAY SPRUCE (*Picea abies* 'Rubra Spicata'). Red new growth in spring changes to red-brown then green. H: 33 ft. (10 m).

ROCKY MOUNTAIN FIR (*Abies lasiocarpa* var. *arizonica* 'Compacta'). Gorgeous blue needles; slow-growing. H: 15 ft. (4.5 m).

SCOTS PINE (*Pinus sylvestris* 'Slim Jim'). Compact form; twisted dark green needles. H: 23 ft. (7 m).

SPREADING JUNIPER
(*Juniperus horizontalis* 'Lime Glow'). Feathery lime foliage. H: 2 ft. (60 cm).
(*J. h.* 'Mother Lode'). Golden foliage holds its colour in part sun. H: 6 in. (15 cm).

WHITE CEDAR (*Thuja occidentalis* 'Lyonsville'). Ball shaped; green foliage. H: 3 ft. (90 cm).

Plants for Hedges and Screens

EVERGREEN

BOXWOOD (*Buxus* spp.). Fine texture; tidy habit; responds well to pruning and part shade. H: 2 to 5 ft. (60 cm. to 1.5 m).

COPPER BEECH (*Fagus sylvatica*). Copper spring and fall colour. H: 70 ft. (20 m).

JUNIPER (*Juniperus* spp.). Soft texture; likes sandy soil. H: 10 to 50 ft. (3 to 15 m).

WHITE CEDAR (*Thuja occidentalis*). Very hardy; needs moist site. H: 30 to 60 ft. (9 to 18 m).

YEW (*Taxus* spp.) Glossy dark needles; tolerates shade; responds well to pruning. H: 10 to 25 ft. (3 to 7.5 m).

DECIDUOUS

ALPINE CURRANT (*Ribes alpinum*). Low-growing; mounding form; takes sun or shade. H: 2 ft. (60 cm).

AMUR PRIVET (*Ligustrum amurense*). Very hardy; best kept clipped. H: 15 ft. (4.5 m).

BLUE ARCTIC WILLOW (*Salix purpurea*). Blue-green leaves; takes part shade. H: 6 ft. (1.8 m).

RED OSIER DOGWOOD (*Cornus sericea*). Brilliant red stems; small dull white flowers and fruit in summer; tolerates moist conditions. H: 6 ft. (1.8 m).

TALL SHRUBS FOR SCREENING

BEAUTYBUSH (*Kolkwitzia amabilis*). Arching habit; pink flowers in late spring. H: 10 ft. (3 m).

RED-LEAF ROSE (*Rosa glauca*, syn. *R. rubrifolia*). Blue-green leaves; small pink single flowers in early summer; big red rosehips in fall. H: 6 ft. (1.8 m).

SILVER-LEAF DOGWOOD (*Cornus alba* 'Elegantissima'). Variegated leaves; creamy flowers in late spring; red bark; tolerates shade. H: 10 ft. (3 m).

VIBURNUM (*Viburnum* x *pragense*). White flowers in spring; handsome foliage. H: 10 ft. (3 m).

Selecting Roses
(see page 101)

ROSE

(*Rosa* 'Blanc Double de Coubert'). Fragrant white repeat bloomer. H: 5 ft. (1.5 m).

(*R. gallica* var. *officinalis* 'Versicolor'). Old variety often called Rosa mundi; deep pink blooms splashed with white in summer. H: 3 ft. (90 cm).

(*R.* 'Winnipeg Parks'). Bushy shrub rose; recurrent bloom. H: 28 in. (70 cm).

Selecting Vines
(see page 103)

CLEMATIS

(*C.* 'Jackmanii'). Large purple blooms in summer. H: 10 ft. (3 m).

Large-flowered hybrids such as 'Niobe' (wine red), 'Comtesse de Bouchaud' (pink) and 'Henryi' (white) bloom in summer. H: 6 to 10 ft. (1.8 to 3 m).

(*C. montana*, *C. macropetala* and *C. alpina*). Bloom in spring in shades of white, pink, blue and mauve. H: 10 to 20 ft. (3 to 6 m).

(*C. terniflora*). Cascades of white flowers in fall. H: 15 to 20 ft. (4.5 to 6 m).

(*C. viticella* 'Betty Corning'). Fragrant lilac bells in summer. H: 6 ft. (1.8 m).

CLIMBING HYDRANGEA (*Hydrangea petiolaris*). Creamy lace-cap flowers in early summer; shade-tolerant; vigorous grower. H: 60 ft. (18 m).

IVY (*Hedera* spp.) Ideal to cover chain-link fence.

JAPANESE HYDRANGEA VINE

(*Schizophragma hydrangeoides*). Elegant look; white flowers in summer; tolerates shade. H: 40 ft. (12 m).

(*S. h.* 'Moonlight'). Foliage has silvery sheen; white flowers in summer; tolerates shade. H: 30 ft. (9 m).

TRUMPET VINE (*Campsis*). Intense scarlet tubular flowers; attracts hummingbirds. H: 30 ft. (9 m). Seeds around.

VIRGINIA CREEPER (*Parthenocissus quinquefolia*). Fabulous fall colour; rapid grower; takes part shade. H: 50 ft. (15 m).

Selecting Anchor Plants
(see page 81)

ANGELICA (*Angelica gigas*). Huge leaves; large purple blooms in late summer or early fall. H: 6 ft. (1.8 m).

ASTILBOIDES (*Astilboides tabularis*). Giant lobed leaves; creamy flowers in early summer; needs moist soil in shade or part shade. H: 5 ft. (1.5 m).

BEAR'S BREECHES (*Acanthus mollis*). White and purple flowers in summer attract bees; drought tolerant. H: 5 ft. (1.5 m).

MULLEIN (*Verbascum* spp.). Grey felt leaves; tall flower spikes, usually yellow in summer. H: 4 to 7 ft. (1.2 to 2.1 m).

RODGERSIA (*Rodgersia aesculifolia*). Chestnut-like leaves; fluffy white flowers in summer; part shade. H: 6 ft. (1.8 m).

Selecting Ornamental Grasses
(see page 104)

Small (less than 2 ft./60 cm)

BLUE FESCUE (*Festuca glauca* 'Boulder Blue' and *F. g.* 'Elijah Blue'). Strong blue colour; spiky form.

BLUE OAT GRASS (*Helictotrichon sempervirens*). Steely blue narrow blades.

GOLDEN JAPANESE FOREST GRASS (*Hakonechloa macra* 'Aureola'). Gold-green striped leaves; cascading habit; copes with sun or shade.

GOLDEN MILLET GRASS (*Milium effusum* 'Aureum'). Bright

yellow leaves in spring; tolerates shade.
JAPANESE BLOOD GRASS (*Imperata cylindrica* 'Red Baron').
Rich red blades; needs well-drained soil.
SEDGE
(*Carex conica* 'Hime-kan-suge', also called 'Snowline').
White-edged blades; tidy habit; needs moisture.
(*C. dolichostachya* 'Gold Fountains'). Slender gold-
edged leaves; needs moisture.
(*C. morrowii* 'Ice Dance'). Cream and green striped
leaves; needs moisture; tolerates shade.

Medium (2 to 4 ft./60 to 120 cm)

EULALIA GRASS
(*Miscanthus sinensis* var. *purpurascens*). Red-orange
fall colour.
(*M. s.* 'Morning Light'). White-margined blades.
FEATHER GRASS (*Stipa tenuissima*). Fine texture; excellent
container annual.
HAIR GRASS (*Deschampsia cespitosa* 'Schottland'). Feathery
texture; takes part shade.
NORTHERN SEA OATS (*Chasmanthium latifolium*). Decorative
seed heads; shade-tolerant; prolific self-seeder.
PURPLE FOUNTAIN GRASS (*Pennisetum setaceum* 'Rubrum').
Maroon-purple leaves; bottlebrush flowers; excellent
container annual.
SWITCH GRASS
(*Panicum virgatum* 'Dallas Blues'). Coarse texture;
powdery blue foliage.
(*P. v.* 'Heavy Metal'). Grey-blue foliage; slow-spreading.
(*P. v.* 'Prairie Sky'). Wide blue blades.

Large (over 4 feet/120 cm)

EULALIA GRASS
(*Miscanthus sinensis* 'Gracillimus'). Narrow leaves with
white midrib; coppery plumes in fall.
(*M. floridulus* syn. *M. giganteus*). Coarse texture; large
white plumes in fall.
(*M. s.* 'Huron Sunrise'). Purple-red plumes in fall.
(*M. s.* 'Silberfeder'). Pinky brown plumes in fall; good
screening plant.
FEATHER REED GRASS (*Calamagrostis* x *acutiflora*
'Avalanche'). Elegant white-striped leaves; silvery plumes
in late summer; tolerates poor soil.
HARDY PAMPAS GRASS (*Saccharum ravennae* syn. *Erianthus
ravennae*). Thick stems; large cream plumes in fall.
PURPLE MOOR GRASS (*Molinia arundinacea* 'Karl Foerster').
Elegant wiry stems; airy plumes in late summer; tolerates
clay soil.

Bamboo

BLACK BAMBOO (*Phyllostachys nigra*). Green foliage and
black stems; needs protection from wind. H: 30 ft. (9 m).
DWARF WHITE-STRIPE BAMBOO (*Pleioblastus fortunei* 'Little
Zebra'). Green and white leaves; vigorous groundcover.
H: 2 to 3 ft. (60 to 90 cm).
FOUNTAIN BAMBOO (*Fargesia nitida*). Clumping form; slow-
growing; prefers shade. H: 10 ft. (3 m).

Selecting Ground Covers
(see page 105)

BUGLEWEED (*Ajuga* x *tenorii* 'Valfredda' syn. *A.* 'Chocolate
Chip'). Copper brown leaves; blue flowers in spring.
H: 4 in. (10 cm).
CHAMOMILE (*Chamaemelum nobile*). Mat-forming; ferny
leaves; needs mowing once a year; deer-resistant. H: 6 to
12 in. (15 to 30 cm).
GOLDEN CREEPING JENNY (*Lysimachia nummularia* 'Aurea').
Golden foliage in part shade or sun; white flowers in early
summer. H: 2 in. (5 cm).
IRISH MOSS (*Sagina subulata*). Moss-like perennial; starry
white flowers in summer. H: 2 in. (5 cm).
NEW ZEALAND BRASS BUTTONS (*Leptinella squalida*). Ferny
foliage; yellow button-like flowers in early summer.
H: 6 in. (15 cm).
SIBERIAN BARREN STRAWBERRY (*Waldsteinia ternata*). Semi-
evergreen; yellow flowers in spring; takes sun or shade.
H: 5 in. (12 cm).
SWEET WOODRUFF (*Galium odoratum*). Starry white flowers
in spring; rapid spreader; takes shade. H: 8 to 10 in.
(20 to 25 cm).
WOOLLY THYME (*Thymus pseudolanuginosus*). Fragrant;
silver-grey foliage; takes some foot traffic. H: 2 in. (5 cm).

Selecting Annuals
(see page 107)

CANNA (*Canna*). Tender bulbs; huge leaves; tropical
coloured flowers in red, orange, yellow and pink.
H: 3 to 6 ft. (90 cm to 1.8 m).
CLARY SAGE (*Salvia horminum*). Pink or blue flowers; self-
seeds. H: 15 in. (38 cm).
COLEUS (*Solenostemon scutellarioides*). Varied textures;
foliage colours from green, yellow, orange to red,
burgundy and black; tolerates shade; fabulous in pots.
H: 8 to 36 in. (20 to 90 cm).

FLOWERING TOBACCO (*Nicotiana alata*). Fragrant white tubular flowers. H: 4 ft. (1.2 m).

FORGET-ME-NOTS (*Myosotis* spp.). Blue or pink flowers in spring; self-seeds. H: 4 to 12 in. (10 to 30 cm).

HONEY BUSH (*Melianthus major*). Huge toothed silver-green leaves; H: 10 ft. (3 m).

Selecting Bulbs
(see page 108)

The following are all spring blooming.

Little Bulbs

ALLIUM (*Allium* spp.). Ball-shaped flowers in purple, pink, blue and white. H. 6 in. to 4 ft. (15 cm to 1.2 m).

DWARF BULBOUS IRIS (*Iris reticulata*). Blue or purple flowers. H: 6 in. (15 cm).

FRITILLARY
(*F. meleagris*). Checkered maroon or plain cream bell-like flowers. H: 12 in. (30 cm).
(*F. persica*). Scented black flowers in late spring. H: 3 ft. (90 cm).

GLORY-OF-THE-SNOW (*Chionodoxa* spp.). Blue flowers; early blooming; will naturalize. H: 5 in. (12 cm).

GRAPE HYACINTH (*Muscari* spp.). Purple spiky flowers; grassy foliage; squirrel-resistant. H: 4 to 8 in. (10 to 20 cm).

SNOWDROP (*Galanthus nivalis*). Very early blooming; scented white bells; will naturalize. H: 6 in. (15 cm).

SPECIES TULIP
(*Tulipa linifolia*). Bright red blooms. H: 6 in. (15 cm).
(*T. tarda*). White and yellow petals; will naturalize. H: 5 in. (12 cm).
(*T. tubergeniana*). Scarlet blooms. H: 8 in. (20 cm).
(*T. turkestanica*). Clusters of dangling white flowers. H: 10 in. (30 cm).

SPRING SNOWFLAKE (*Leucojum vernum*). Resembles a giant snowdrop; tolerates wet soil. H: 1 ft. (30 cm).

WINTER ACONITE (*Eranthis hyemalis*). Very early blooming; yellow flowers; soak tubers before planting. H: 3 in. (8 cm).

Big Bulbs

DAFFODIL
(*Narcissus* 'Ice Follies'). White with pale yellow trumpet. H: 15 in. (38 cm).
(*N.* 'Minnow'). White and yellow blooms. H: 8 in. (20 cm).
(*N. poeticus*). Curved white petals; orange-red centres.

H: 16 in. (40 cm).
(*N.* 'Thalia'). Multiple flowers on each stem; intense white. H: 9 in. (22 cm).

TULIP
(*Tulipa* 'Angelique'). Scented pink peony-like flowers; opens late. H: 16 in. (40 cm).
(*T.* 'Ballerina'). Glorious stripey orange; lily-flowered. H: 18 in. (45 cm).
(*T.* 'Princess Irene'). Orange with flames of purple; lovely among forget-me-nots. H: 1 ft. (30 cm).

Selecting Plants for Containers
(see page 108)

Trees

JAPANESE MAPLE
(*Acer palmatum* 'Red Dragon'). Finely dissected red leaves hold colour all summer. H: 10 ft. (3 m).
(*A. p.* 'Sango-kaku'). Gold fall foliage; coral-coloured bark. H: 20 ft. (6 m).
(*A. p.* 'Villa Taranto'). Finely dissected green leaves. H: 7 to 10 ft. (2.1 to 3 m).

Perennials

HOSTA
(*Hosta* 'Bitsy Green'). Slender wavy leaves; lavender blooms in summer. H: 6 in. (25 cm).
(*H.* 'Blue Jay'). Intense blue leaves; lavender flowers in early summer. H: 8 in. (20 cm).
(*H.* 'Elvis Lives'). Wavy blue-green leaves; lavender flowers in early summer. H: 18 in. (45 cm).
(*H.* 'Halcyon'). Thick blue leaves; lavender flowers in summer. H: 16 in. (40 cm).
(*H.* 'Krossa Regal'). Blue-green leaves; lavender flowers in summer. H: 28 in. (70 cm).
(*H.* 'Masquerade'). White-edged leaves; purple flowers in summer. H: 6 in. (15 cm).
(*H.* 'Queen Josephine'). Glossy cream-edged foliage; pale purple flowers in summer. H: 15 in. (38 cm).
(*H.* 'Regal Splendor'). White-edged green leaves; lavender flowers in late summer. H: 30 in. (75 cm).
(*H.* 'Spilt Milk'). Blue-green leaves streaked with cream; pure white flowers in early summer. H: 15 in. (38 cm).
(*H.* 'Tattoo'). Rounded gold leaves with green markings; lavender flowers in early summer. H: 10 in. (25 cm).

CORAL BELLS (*Heuchera* spp.). Good filler plants; foliage colours include silver-green, gold, red, copper and burgundy; flowers are white, red or pink and bloom in late spring or early summer. H: 10 to 16 in. (25 to 40 cm).

HENS AND CHICKS (*Sempervivum* spp.). Rosette-forming succulents; take sun and wind. H: 3 to 6 in. (8 to 15 cm).

Japanese painted fern (*Athyrium niponicum* var. *pictum*). Silvery foliage, burgundy stems. H: 15 in. (38 cm).

LADY FERN (*Athyrium filix-femina* var. *angustum* 'Lady in Red'). Mint green leaves; red stems. H: 30 in. (75 cm).

SEDGE

(*Carex morrowii* 'Silver Sceptre'). Silver-margined blades. H: 10 in. (25 cm).

(*C. muskingumensis* 'Oehme'). Yellow-edged leaves. H: 20 in. (50 cm).

Annuals

PLECTRANTHUS (*Plectranthus* 'Mona Lavender'). Green and purple leaves; neon purple flowers. H: 18 in. (45 cm).

SWEET POTATO VINE

(*Ipomoea batatas* 'Blackie'). Trailing annual vine; black leaves.

(*I. b.* 'Marguerite'). Trailing annual vine; chartreuse-gold leaves.

Selecting Plants for Shade
(see page 112)

Shrubs

BOXWOOD (*Buxus* spp.). Evergreen; small leaves; tidy habit. H: 2 to 5 ft. (60 cm. to 1.5 m).

Carolina allspice (*Calycanthus floridus*). Small strawberry-scented flowers in summer; needs rich soil. H: 8 ft. (2.4 m).

CUTLEAF STEPHANANDRA (*Stephanandra incisa*). Thicket-forming; arching shoots; white flowers in early summer. H: 6 ft. (1.8 m).

HEMLOCK

(*Tsuga canadensis* 'Gentsch White'). Evergreen; new growth is white. H: 4 ft. (1.2 m).

(*T. c.* 'Stewart's Gem'). Bun-shaped dwarf evergreen. H: 2 ft. (60 cm).

RHODODENDRON

(*Rhododendron auriculatum*). Scented white flowers; blooms in late spring or early summer. H: 8 to 15 ft. (2.4 to 4.5 m).

(*R.* 'Catawbiense Album'). Large leaves; white flowers in late spring. H: 10 ft. (3 m).

(*R.* 'PJM'). Little-leaf form; hardy; rosy purple flowers in

spring. H: 4 ft. (1.2 m).

(*R.* 'Ramapo'). Little-leaf form; purple blooms in spring. H: 2 ft. (60 cm).

(*R. yakushimanum*). Fuzzy leaves; pale pink flowers in spring. H: 3 ft. (90 cm).

SNOWBERRY (*Symphoricarpos albus* var. *laevigatus*). Pink flowers in summer; white fruit. H: 6 ft. (1.8 m).

WINTERBERRY (*Ilex verticillata* 'Sparkleberry'). Red berries in winter. H: 12 ft. (3.6 m).

YEW (*Taxus* spp.). Evergreen; glossy green needles; takes pruning. H: 10 to 25 ft. (3 to 7.5 m).

Perennials

BLACK SNAKEROOT (*Actaea simplex* syn. *Cimicifuga* 'Black Negligee'). Lacy black foliage; wands of white flowers in late summer. H: 4 ft. (1.5 m).

BRUNNERA (*Brunnera* 'Jack Frost'). Heart-shaped silver leaves; small blue flowers in spring. H: 1 ft. (30 cm).

CHRISTMAS FERN (*Polystichum acrostichoides*). Evergreen leathery fronds. H: 18 in. (45 cm).

CORAL BELLS (*Heuchera* 'Lime Rickey'). Chartreuse foliage; ivory flowers in late spring. H: 8 in. (20 cm).

DOGTOOTH VIOLET (*Erythronium* spp.). Spring ephemeral (blooms early then goes dormant); yellow, pink or white flowers. H: 6 to 14 in. (15 to 35 cm).

FOAMFLOWER (*Tiarella* spp.). Fluffy cream or pink flowers; woodland groundcover. H: 8 to 12 in. (20 to 30 cm).

GERANIUM (*Geranium pratense* 'Hocus Pocus'). Chocolate leaves; lavender flowers bloom all summer. H: 16 in. (40 cm).

HELLEBORE

(*Helleborus niger*). White blooms in winter. H: 1 ft. (30 cm).

(*H. x sternii*). Pinkish green flowers in early spring. H: 14 in. (35 cm).

(*H. viridis*). Long-lasting green flowers in spring. H: 16 in. (40 cm).

HOSTA (*Hosta* spp.). See pages 162 and 171.

JAPANESE PAINTED FERN (*Athyrium niponicum* var. *pictum*). Silvery foliage, burgundy stems. H: 15 in. (38 cm).

LICORICE FERN (*Polypodium glycyrrhiza*). Down-curving fronds. H: 1 ft. (30 cm).

LIGULARIA (*Ligularia* 'Britt-Marie Crawford'). Shiny purple-maroon leaves; coarse orange flowers in late summer. H: 3 ft. (80 cm).

LUNGWORT (*Pulmonaria* 'Excalibur'). Green-edged silver leaves; pink and blue flowers in spring. H: 1 ft. (30 cm).

MALE FERN (*Dryopteris felix-mas*). Light green fronds. H: 3 ft. (90 cm).

<u>SOLOMON'S SEAL</u> (*Polygonatum multiflorum*). Arching stems; dangling white flowers in spring. H: 3 ft. (90 cm).
<u>TRILLIUM</u> (*Trillium* spp.). Spring ephemeral; white sometimes yellow or red flowers. H: 5 to 20 in. (12 to 50 cm).

Selecting Native Plants
(see page 114)

Shrubs

<u>FOUR-WING SALTBUSH</u> (*Atriplex canescens*). Silver foliage. H: 6 ft. (1.8 m).
<u>RED OSIER DOGWOOD</u> (*Cornus sericea*). Red stems; small dull white flowers and fruit in summer; tolerates wet sites. H: 6 ft. (1.8 m).
<u>SERVICEBERRY</u> (*Amelanchier*). See page 171.
<u>SILVER SAGEBRUSH</u> (*Artemisia cana*). Silver leaves. H: 5 ft. (1.5 m).
<u>SPICE BUSH</u> (*Lindera benzoin*). Tiny yellow flowers in spring. H: 10 ft. (3 m).

Perennials

<u>BIG BLUESTEM</u> (*Andropogon gerardii*). Large grass; loves moist soil and sun. H: 6 ft. (1.8 m).
<u>BLACK-EYED SUSAN</u> (*Rudbeckia hirta*). Glowing yellow daisy-like flowers in late summer. H: 1 to 3 ft. (30 to 90 cm).
<u>BLANKET FLOWERS</u> (*Gaillardia* spp.). Red or orange or gold daisy-like blooms in summer. H: 1 to 3 ft. (30 to 90 cm).
<u>CONEFLOWER</u> (all are drought-tolerant)
 (*Echinacea angustifolia*). Rosy blooms in early summer. H: 4 ft. (1.2 m).
 (*E. pallida*). Linear leaves; pink flowers in summer. H: 4 ft. (1.2 m).
 (*E. purpurea*). Deep pink petals around a conical brown disk in midsummer. H: 5 ft. (1.5 m).
 (*E. p.* 'Hope'). Pale pink blooms in midsummer. H: 30 in. (75 cm).
 (*E. p.* 'Razzmatazz'). Pink double flowers in summer. H: 30 in. (75 cm).
 (*E. p.* 'Sunrise'). Citron yellow flowers in summer. H: 3 ft. (90 cm).
 (*E. p.* 'Sunset'). Orange-salmon blooms in summer. H: 30 in. (75 cm).
<u>GOLDENROD</u> (does not cause allergies)
 (*Solidago* 'Golden Wings'). Yellow blooms in late summer. H: 4 ft. (1.2 m).
 (*S.* 'Cloth of Gold'). Dwarf cultivar; golden flowers in late summer. H: 1 ft. (30 cm).

<u>JOE PYE WEED</u>
 (*Eupatorium fistulosum*). Huge rosy blooms in late summer; attracts butterflies. H: 8 ft. (2.4 m).
 (*E. maculatum* 'Atropurpureum'). Dark purple stalks; dark pink flowers in late summer. H: 6 ft. (1.8 m).
<u>LANCE-LEAF COREOPSIS</u> (*Coreopsis lanceolata*). Sunny yellow meadow flower; blooms in summer. H: 3 ft. (90 cm).
Prairie smoke (*Geum triflorum*). Rosy purple flowers in early spring; feathery pink seed heads. H: 6 in. (15 cm).
<u>WILD BEE BALM</u> (*Monarda fistulosa*). Lilac and pink flowers in summer. H: 4 ft. (1.2 m).

Selecting Plants for Autumn Colour
(see page 115)

Shrubs

<u>OAKLEAF HYDRANGEA</u> (*Hydrangea quercifolia*). Large cream flowers in late summer; wine red fall foliage; exfoliating bark. H: 6 ft. (1.8 m).
<u>REDVEIN ENKIANTHUS</u> (*Enkianthus campanulatus*). Pink bell-like blooms in spring; flaming autumn foliage; likes slightly acid soil. H: 10 ft. (3 m).

Perennials

<u>BOLTONIA</u> (*Boltonia asteroides*). Clouds of small white flowers. H: 6 ft. (1.8 m).
<u>JAPANESE ANEMONE</u> (*Anemone x hybrida* 'Honorine Jobert'). Clear white flowers; takes part shade. H: 5 ft. (1.5 m).
<u>PHLOX</u> (*Phlox* 'David'). White flowers; mildew-resistant. H: 40 in. (1 m).
<u>TOAD LILY</u> (*Tricyrtis* spp.). Small orchid-like flowers; takes part shade. H: 12 to 32 in. (30 to 80 cm).
<u>YELLOW WAX BELLS</u> (*Kirengeshoma koreana*). Maple-like leaves; pale yellow bell-shaped flowers; takes part shade. H: 3 ft. (90 cm).

Bulbs

<u>AUTUMN CROCUS</u> (*Colchicum autumnale*). Pinky purple blooms. H: 7 in. (17 cm).

Selecting Trees for Winter Interest
(see page 116)

<u>MAACKIA</u> (*Maackia amurensis*). Exfoliating bark; new foliage in spring is silver. H: 50 ft. (15 m).

Bibliography

PAPERBARK MAPLE (*Acer griseum*). Red-orange fall colour; cinnamon peeling bark. H: 30 ft. (9 m).
SEVEN-SON FLOWER (*Heptacodium miconioides*). Creamy fragrant flowers in late summer or early fall; exfoliating bark. H: 20 ft. (6 m).

My Ten Essential Plants
(see page 118)

BLACK ELDER (*Sambucus* 'Black Lace'). Shrub; cutleaf purple-black foliage; pink flowers in early summer; black berries. H: 8 to 10 ft. (2.4 to 3 m).
BLACK SNAKEROOT (*Actaea simplex* syn. *Cimicifuga* 'James Compton'). Perennial; deep purple-brown leaves; white bottlebrush blooms in late summer. H: 32 in. (80 cm).
BOWMAN'S ROOT (*Gillenia trifoliata*). Native perennial; starry white flowers in June; takes sun or shade. H: 3 ft. (90 cm).
GOLDEN JAPANESE FOREST GRASS (*Hakonechloa macra* 'Aureola'). Cascading grass; yellow striped blades; takes sun or shade. H: 10 in. (25 cm).
HOSTA (*Hosta* 'June'). Perennial; blue-edged leaves have cream centres that change to chartreuse as the season progresses; violet flowers in midsummer; shade. H: 15 in. (38 cm).
JAPANESE MAPLE (*Acer palmatum* 'Dissectum Atropurpureum'). Low-growing, wide-spreading tree; fine texture; neon orange fall foliage. H: 8 to 10 ft. (2.4 to 3 m).
LARGE MERRYBELLS (*Uvularia grandiflora*). Native woodland perennial; lily-like yellow blooms in May. H: 2 ft. (60 cm).
SERVICEBERRY (*Amelanchier canadensis*). Small native tree; white flowers in spring; red berries in summer; scarlet foliage in fall; grey bark in winter. H: 21 ft. (6.3 m).
VIBURNUM (*Viburnum plicatum* 'Summer Snowflake'). Versatile shrub for sun or shade; white lace-cap flowers all summer. H: 4 to 7 ft. (1.2 to 2.1 m).
WHITE SNAKEROOT (*Eupatorium rugosum* 'Chocolate'). Perennial with purple-chocolate foliage all summer; white flowers in fall. H: 4 ft. (1.2 m).

The following books offer detailed information on some of the topics covered in *How to Make a Garden*.

Allison, James. *Water in the Garden.* North Vancouver: Whitecap Books, 2004.

Fell, Derek. *An Encyclopedia of Garden Design & Structure: Ideas and Inspiration for Your Garden.* Richmond Hill: Firefly Books, 2005.

Fryberger, Betsy G. *The Changing Garden: Four Centuries of European and American Art.* California: Stanford University Press, 2003.

Harris, Marjorie. *Botanica North America: The Illustrated Guide to Our Native Plants, Their Botany, History, and the Way They Have Shaped Our World.* New York: HarperCollins, 2003.

Harris, Marjorie. *Pocket Gardening.* Toronto: HarperCollins Canada, 2004.

Hayward, Gordon. *Garden Paths: Inspiring Designs and Practical Projects.* Charlotte, Vermont: Camden House, 1993.

Joyce, David. *Pruning and Training Plants: The Complete Guide.* Richmond Hill: Firefly Books, 2001.

Murfitt, Rex. *Creating and Planting Alpine Gardens.* Wayne, Pennsylvania: Mackey Books, 2005.

Pope, Nori and Sandra. *Colour by Design.* San Francisco: SOMA Books, 1998.

Starcher, Allison Mia. *Good Bugs for Your Garden.* New York: Algonquin Books, 1995.

Van Sweden, James and Wolfgang Oehme. *Gardening with Nature.* New York: Random House, New York, 1997.

Verey, Rosemary. *Classic Garden Design: How to Adapt and Recreate Garden Features of the Past.* New York: Random House, 1989.

Acknowledgements

Picture Credits

Thanks to Margot Belanger, Karen Steed and Juliet Mannock who dished out the advice and provided the cheerleading. Thanks to everyone who has made working at *Gardening Life* magazine and the *Globe and Mail* such a great experience, and to all those wonderful people who have let me interview them over the years: Michael Pellegrino and Shawn Gibson of Teatro Verde; Darren and Michael Schmaal of The Copper Leaf; landscape architect Janet Rosenberg; Carol Cowan; Ted Johnston; Frank Cabot; Brigid Allen; Derek Welsh of Authentic Tree Care; Martin Ciconne and Michael Renaud of Horticultural Design; Paul Zammit of Plant World; Tom Hobbs of Southlands Nursery; Miriam Goldberger of Wildflower Farm; Margaret Serreo of Fiesta Gardens, Tom Intven of Canadale Nurseries; Pam Bingham of Luna Landscape Lighting; Kent Ford of Kent Ford Designs; John Valleau of Heritage Perennials; Tim Wood of Spring Meadow Nurseries; Linda Leggett of Via Verde; Peter Cantley of Loblaws; Larry Davidson of Lost Horizons; Muriel Neale of Bluestem Nursery; Jim Lounsbery of Vineland Nurseries; Wendy Woodworth of Spadina House; and Gerry Cornwell.

And thanks to those who have helped make my garden into a paradise: Reinhard Reitzenstein and Olga Korper of the Olga Korper Gallery: for the glorious fountain sculpture; Pam Bingham of Luna Landscape Lighting for the great lighting; James Dale of Earth Inc. for the garden revival; and Lisa Rapaport and Elysse Shelley of Plant Architect for the magnificent four-season room. And to Esther Giroux, Zenon Mandziuk and Stephen McClare for helping to keep the garden perfect.

My gratitude also goes to Sheree-Lee Olson, who's been my editor and good friend at the *Globe and Mail* all these years; Karen York, dear friend and ace editor who knows everything about plants and so is a botanical editor supreme; Katie Dupuis for her hard work organizing the photo acquisitions for the book; Amy Hick for her editorial help; Fidel Peña and Claire Dawson of Underline Studio who created the wonderful design for this book; Prashant Miranda for his incredible illustrations; Sara Angel of Angel Editions who conceived and produced this book; and Anne Collins and Stacey Cameron of Random House Canada who have been so kind and helpful.

Index

How to Make a Garden is an
Angel Edition created under the
editorial and creative direction
of Sara Angel

BOOK DESIGN
Underline Studio

EDITOR
Karen York

PROJECT EDITOR
Amy Hick

ASSISTANT EDITOR;
PHOTO RESEARCH AND ACQUISITION
Katie Dupuis

COPY EDITOR
Sarah Davies

INDEX
Laurie Coulter

Essential planting tips :

- READ PLANT TAGS CAREFULLY • SOAK PLANTS WELL BEFORE IN
- CUT OFF BROKEN STEMS ON WOODY PLANTS • TRIM MUSHY ROOTS
  BARE ROOT PLANTS • PLANT WHEN IT'S COOL • WATER WELL
  TIME • MULCH QUICKLY •

How do I make my garden attractive in the winter?

To do today :
* Turn the comp
* Weed
* Water early in the
* Change water in
* Dead head •
* Prune the vines

A CONTEMPLATIVE GARDEN WOULD BE PEACEFUL •
I NEVER THOUGHT TO PLANT A GARDEN AT THE
COTTAGE
AN EVENING GARDEN WOULD BE PERFECT FOR
ENTERTAINING

CAN I A
A PROFESSIO
THINGS ?

To do today :
* Turn the compost
* Weed
* Water early in the morning
* Change water in the birdbath
* Dead head •
* Prune the vines on the pergola

When choosing plants, colour
is very important. Blues,
purples, & greens for instance,
are considered cool colours,
& have a calming effect.
From purply-indigo to
pale azure, the blues make
beautiful music on their
own or accompanying other
hues •

Rosa ru

Acer jap

Lilium 'Ca

Euphorbia a

Halesia e

A CONTEMPLATIVE GAR
I NEVER THOUGHT TO
COTT
AN EVENING GARDEN
ENTER